Waterfronts in Post-industrial Cities

Waterfronts in Post-industrial Cities

Edited by Richard Marshall

170201

SPON PRESS
Taylor & Francis Group

London and New York

First published 2001
by Spon Press
11 New Fetter Lane, London EC4P 4EE

Simultaneously published in the USA and Canada
by Spon Press
29 West 35th Street, New York, NY 10001

Spon Press is an imprint of the Taylor & Francis Group

Typeset in Frutiger Light by Wearset, Boldon, Tyne and Wear
Printed and bound in Great Britain by St Edmundsbury Press,
Bury St Edmunds, Suffolk

British Library Cataloguing in Publication Data
A catalogue record for this book is available from the British Library

Library of Congress Cataloging in Publication Data
Waterfronts in post industrial cities / edited by Richard Marshall.
    p. cm.
    Includes index.
    1. Urban renewal. 2. Waterfronts. I. Marshall, Richard, 1967–
HT170 .W38 2001
307.3'4–dc21

                                                    00–066144

ISBN 0-415-25516-3

Contents

Illustration credits

The editor and the publishers would like to thank the following individuals and institutions for giving permission to reproduce illustrations. We have made every effort to contact copyright holders, but if any errors have been made we would be happy to correct them at a later printing.

Bruttomesso, Rinio   3.1–3.4
Casariego, Joaquin and Elsa Guerra   7.7, 7.10, 7.11
Elliott, Sara   4.1, 4.7, 4.16, 9.6–9.9, 9.16, 9.18
Genoa Port Authority   7.1, 7.3, 7.4, 7.8, 7.15, 7.16
Guggenheim Museum, Bilbao   Cover photograph
Loeb Library Special Collections, Harvard Graduate School of Design   9.11
Murbach, David   9.1, 9.5, 9.12, 9.13
Pride-Wells, Michaele   9.4, 9.10, 9.14, 9.15, 9.17
Richard Marshall   2.1, 2.11–2.14, 2.16–2.17, 4.5–4.6, 4.10–4.12, 4.18–4.19
Sant 'Anna, Victor   4.3, 4.8
Skidmore Owings and Merrill LLP   4.13–4.15
Suzuki, Yuri   4.9, 4.17, 7.6, 7.9, 7.12–7.14
Taller de Ideas/Alfonso Vegara   6.1–6.2
Vancouver City Planning Department   2.3, 2.5–2.10, 2.15
Waikeen Ng   6.3

Acknowledgements

This work is the result of the hard work and dedication of many people. The editor is grateful to the contributors for their efforts and patience.

Special mention must be made to several people at the Harvard Design School, including Dean Peter Rowe, Associate Dean Russell Sanna and Professor Alex Krieger, for their support and assistance both with the staging of the waterfront conference and for this publication. Thanks must also go to Corlette McCoy and her staff at the Harvard Design School Office of Executive Education.

The editor would like to thank the participants of the waterfront conference: Alderman Duco Stadig, President Josu Bergara Etxebarria, Juan Ignacio Vidarte, Luis Rodriguez Llopis, Alderman Bruno Gabrielli, Giuliano Gallanti, Mario Coyula, Vice Mayor Juan José Cardona González, Zhang Hui Ming, Professor Zheng Shiling, John Kriken, Lord Mayor Frank Sartor, Councillor Lynne Kennedy and Larry Beasley.

The editor is also grateful to a number of colleagues who helped in the exploration of waterfront ideas, especially Ed Robbins, Lee Cott, Joaquin Casariego, Elsa Guerra and Elizabeth Mossop who acted as partial reviewers of the work in progress.

Thanks to Victor Lai, Pablo Allard, Kimberley Jones and Aki Omi who acted as research assistants through the course of this research.

Finally, I would like to thank my wife Hele for her support and enduring patience; I am eternally grateful.

PART I
INTRODUCTION

1 Contemporary urban space-making at the water's edge

Richard Marshall

In an article devoted to the public realm, Peter Davey, expressing a widely held view, laments that "we have almost forgotten how to build cities" (Davey, 1999:32). This sentiment stems from a common feeling of disappointment toward the contemporary city. Today we find many articles and books that condemn the current condition of our urban environments. Everyone, it seems, is anti-city. However, the condition in which we find ourselves is not an issue of memory. We have not forgotten how cities were made, rather our ideas of what a city is and how to put it together seem at odds with the way the world works today. A nostalgia for earlier times reinforces conceptions of older models of the city. Our cities have changed faster than we have been able to adjust our thinking and because of this the contemporary crisis of public space is due to a lack of confidence in knowing what works today. Our problem is not one of memory; it is one of adjusting our ideas of what is an appropriate urban form to be in line with the current reality of our culture and society. What is needed in urban design today, above all else, is a re-calibration of our ideas to the currency of our time.

The city is becoming less the result of design and more the expression of economic and social forces. The size of contemporary urban agglomerations means that no one single authority controls the form of the city. A mixture of bureaucracy and market forces defines the form of the city. The city is a physical container of our culture and, as such, it is the expression of us. The city is a mirror of the complexity of modern life. The result is a city environment where instability is the only constant. The results of half a century of urban space-making have left us with a diffused urban structure; a city pieced together from heterogeneous elements that when combined create a homogeneous aesthetic. This amorphous city appears abstract, disordered, confused and illogical. This abstraction acts to diffuse meaningful relationships for those that live in the city and inevitably leads us to feelings of loss and a yearning for a better place, for an idealized urban environment.

It is within these present difficulties that a space has opened up in the city which allows expressions of hope for urban vitality. The urban waterfront provides us with this space. On the waterfront, we see glimpses of new city-making paradigms, partial visions for what our cities might be. If the city has come to be regarded as a reflection of society and its problems, it itself is a problem of unprecedented complexity. By focusing on the urban waterfront, we are able to isolate and view in focus specific responses to the problems of disorder and confusion mentioned previously.

Nan Ellin, exploring the idea of postmodern urbanism, notes that among anthropologists, cultural theorists, architects, and urban planners there has developed a fascination with notions of edge, a response "to the dissolution of traditional limits and lines of demarcation due to rapid urbanization and globalization" (Ellin, 1999:4). Among architects and planners, a great deal of attention is being paid to spaces considered interstitial, "terrains vagues," "no man's land," or "ghost wards" (Schwarzer, 1998). Ellin states that this is apparent

> in the concern for designing along national borders and between ecologically-differentiated areas such as along waterfronts . . . The notion that the talents and energies of architects and urban planners should contribute to mending seams, not tearing them asunder, to healing the world, not to salting its wounds, has grown much more widespread in acceptance.
>
> (Ellin, 1999:5)

It is in the spaces provided by the urban waterfront that planners and designers wrestle with the appropriateness of their intentions for the present, and for the future.

The time in which we live is often referred to as postmodern. The rise of postmodernism, in its many forms, is a general desire to reinvest meaning into various aspects of our lives. Today, meaning is central to discussions of the city. This, despite the fact that such discussions have become so contested. The crisis of the public realm that Davey speaks of is really a crisis of meaning. What does the public realm mean in an increasingly global and fragmented world? How do we as designers accommodate multiple meanings in the design of public space? The best types of public space allow for the inclusion of multiple meanings and all levels of society. As Rowe points out, the alternatives are too often exclusive, corporately or authoritarian dominated precincts (Rowe, 1997: 35).

In the articulation of urban waterfronts, these issues are critical. The visibility of these sites means the waterfront becomes the stage upon which the most important pieces are set. In doing so, the waterfront is an expression of what we are as a culture. The urban waterfront provides possibilities to create pieces of city, to paraphrase Davey, that enrich life, offer decency and hope as well as functionality, and can give some notion of the urban ways of living celebrated by Baudelaire and Benjamin, Oscar Wilde and Otto Wagner. In these possibilities, we remember that urban development is not just for profit, or personal aggrandizement, but for the benefit of humanity and the planet as well. It is on the urban waterfront that these visions of the city are finding form. These are the sites of post-industrial city space-making.

The reuse of obsolete industrial space along the waterfront is a major challenge and an opportunity for cities around the world. Some of the most important redevelopments in recent years have been waterfront revitalization projects: consider, for example, such projects as London's Canary Wharf, New York's Battery Park City, Vancouver's Granville Island, Sydney's Darling Harbour, or San Francisco's Mission Bay. Waterfronts, of course, have historically been the staging points for the import and export of goods. Location next to the water was a competitive advantage to many industrial operations. The edge between city and water, between the production site and its transport basing point, was the most intense zone of use in the nineteenth-century city. Use on the urban waterfront was often exclusively port or manufacturing related. The wealth of cities was based on their ability to facilitate the need of industrial capital to access waterfront resources. However, the creation of this wealth brought with it environmental degradation and toxicity, which today characterize these residual urban spaces.

Our information-saturated, service-oriented economic systems no longer rely on the industrial and manufacturing operations of the past. Technological changes have redefined the relationships of transport and industry. The concurrent advancements of road, rail and water transport, combined with the requirements of containerization, have shifted the basing points for global water transport away from previously historic waterfronts. With this passing, the relationship between water and the generators of economic wealth has changed. Typically, these areas exist as spaces of urban redundancy, as left over spaces in the city. The use and the environmental condition of these spaces are of major concern to many cities in their revitalization efforts.

These waterfront redevelopment projects speak to our future, and to our past. They speak to a past based in industrial production, to a time of tremendous growth and expansion, to social and economic structures that no longer exist, to a time when environmental degradation was an unacknowledged by-product of growth and profit. Through historical circumstance, these sites are immediately adjacent to centers of older cities and, typically, are separated from the physical, cultural and psychological connections that exist in every city. They speak to a future by providing opportunities for cities to reconnect with their water's edge. Because of their size and complexity, these sites require innovative mechanisms for their consolidation. Historically the sites of industry, they now attempt to re-center activity in urban space, to reposition concentrations of activity, to shift the focus from the old to the new.

Waterfronts have been a topic of academic and professional interest since the 1960s. The success of projects such as the Inner Harbor in Baltimore spawned a series of large urban redevelopment projects on waterfront sites around the world. Waterfronts became associated with ways to recreate the image of a city, to recapture economic investment and to attract people back to deserted downtowns. Waterfront development has generated its own discipline. As Meyer notes, "professionals (and academics) from all over the world keep one another informed of the most recent developments by means of international waterfront networks" (Meyer, 1999: 13). The Waterfront Center, based in Washington, DC, Centro Internazionale Città d'Acqua in Venice, and the Association

Internationale Villes et Ports in Le Havre are three examples. These networks produce their own publications and hold their own conferences. An indication of how "competitive" this industry has become is that on the same weekend in October of 1999 three waterfront conferences occurred in North America alone. These were "Waterfronts in Post-Industrial Cities," held in Cambridge by the Harvard Graduate School of Design; "Urban Waterfronts 17," held in Charleston by the Waterfront Center, and "Worldwide Urban Waterfronts," held in Vancouver by Baltic Conventions from the United Kingdom.

The urban waterfront tells us many things about the way we make, and think about, cities. Projects such as the London Docklands are examples of how planning and design intentions are subverted by the concerns of power and capital (Malone, 1996: 15). Sydney's Darling Harbour is an example of a politically driven project that circumvented city and state regulatory systems to satisfy political agendas. Some have described the project as an "ill conceived insertion of gigantic new developments" into the fabric of the city (Morrison, 1991:4). Amsterdam's Ij-Oevers project is an example of a project that speculated heavily on global financial growth, which did not eventuate. Such projects teach us about the volatility of markets and global capital. They also teach us about the nature of building cities and how to plan for their construction. Projects such as Boston's Fan Pier or Melbourne's Docklands are current manifestations that deal with issues of public access and the appropriate mix of uses on privileged waterfront sites.

Large waterfront redevelopment projects often circumvent regulatory systems, and can be so insular as to deny the existence of the context into which they insert themselves. They reside in a self-imposed vacuum. However, their presence often puts pressure on existing infrastructure, on highways, and road systems. The availability of new tracts of very large land allows for programs, often at odds with the scale and grain of the traditional city, to find places to locate. These are the sites for big program facilities such as museums, exhibition halls, convention centers and sports stadiums.

There is a tendency, in much of the literature, to view waterfronts as a kind of urban panacea, a cure-all for ailing cities in search of new self-images or ways of dealing with issues of competition for capital developments or tourist dollars. The waterfront redevelopment project has became synonymous with visions of exuberance. Images of Baltimore's Inner Harbor, or of Sydney's Darling Harbour (or any number of others), filled with joyous masses, inspired city officials and urban planners around the world and led to a rash of "festival marketplaces." However, the focus on the end-product of waterfront development ignores the problems, and possibilities, faced by cities as they work to create them. The idea of project-as-product combined with the spread of "architectural capital" has led to situations where international design clichés characterize the waterfronts of Boston, Tokyo and Dublin (Malone, 1996: 263). The result is a kind of rubber-stamping of the "successful" waterfront magic, often with limited results.

This type of thinking deals with such developments removed from the political structures and financial mechanisms that are fundamental to their realization. These projects, however, are born out of a process, one that involves all levels of government, significant sources of capital, various organizations and individuals that may all have competitive agendas. In the consideration of waterfront projects, one must understand the peculiarities of the contexts and their relationship to international frameworks. Only in this way can understandings from one situation be applicable as lessons to another.

The factors that have led to these waterfront opportunities are well known. These have combined to create sites of abandonment. These sites, being adjacent to water, now offer us unique opportunities. However, as Malone points out, neither the factors that have created the opportunities for redevelopment nor the processes of renewal fall outside the common frameworks for urban development. The urban waterfront is, simply stated, a new frontier for conventional development process (Malone, 1996: 2). Both the types of development and the forms of capital on the contemporary waterfront are common to other parts of the city. What makes the contemporary urban waterfront interesting is the high visibility of this form of development. The high profile of their locations means that waterfront projects are magnified intersections of a number of urban forces. Simply, the economic and political stakes (and hence the design stakes) are higher on the urban waterfront. Indeed, through changes in technology and economics and the shifting of industrial occupancies, the waterfront has become a tremendous opportunity to create environments that reflect contemporary ideas of the city, society and culture.

In October 1999, a group of political leaders, mayors, city councilors, heads of planning, architects, planners, and financiers, from eight international cities, met with faculty from the Harvard Graduate School of Design for a three-day conference entitled, "Waterfronts in Post Industrial Cities." The participating cities were Amsterdam, Bilbao, Genoa, Havana, Las Palmas de Gran Canaria, Shanghai, Sydney, and Vancouver. The aim of the conference was twofold: to explore the challenges faced by these cities in dealing with development on their waterfronts, and to place those considerations into a larger understanding of contemporary urbanism.

Most books on waterfronts deal with a relatively narrow collection of cities and projects – London, New York, Toronto, Barcelona, etc. One might describe them as the "top ten list" of waterfront revitalization stories. Boston and Baltimore, for example, are now the stuff of waterfront redevelopment legend. Our aim in developing the conference was to explore two types of "waterfront city." The first type of city can be found in other publications. Our aim, however, was to retell their stories to understand not only the successes but also the challenges faced by these cities – Amsterdam, Genoa, Sydney and Vancouver – in their revitalization efforts. The second type of city was much harder to determine and does not, or minimally, appear in the waterfront literature. Our aim in selecting these cities was to find contemporary examples that represent the emerging contexts for waterfront revitalization efforts – these include Bilbao, Havana, Las Palmas de Gran Canaria and Shanghai. Our intention was to move beyond the glamour of these revitalization efforts to evaluate their success, understand the challenges that were overcome, and reflect on the longer-term sustainability of the projects in social and economic terms. Our goal was also to try to uncover lessons from the first type of city that can be applied to the second type of city.

The value of the conference was that it allowed decision-makers to engage with planners and designers in a meaningful dialogue. Too often, communication between decision-makers and designers and planners only occurs after major decisions have already been made. The aim of the conference was to open a dialogue and create possibilities for more engaging and informed discussions. The conference advocated an inclusive approach that engages designers, politicians, developers, and economists. The central question for all of us is what is an appropriate urbanity as we start a new millennium. The urban waterfront is an ideal setting for these considerations. This book is an exploration of these visions.

The title of the conference and this book is worth explaining. Borrowing the definition from Savitch, post-industrialism refers to a broad phenomenon that encompasses changes in what we do for a living, how we do it, and where it occurs (Savitch, 1988). Specifically, the post-industrial city deals with processing and services rather than manufacturing, intellectual capacity rather than muscle power, and dispersed office environments rather than concentrated factories. These changes manifest themselves into the building of a new physical environment constructed specifically to meet the needs of the twenty-first century. Examining the redevelopment of the urban waterfront tells us a lot about what we as a culture believe those needs to be.

Urban waterfront developments are no different to other forms of redevelopment in the sense that they cover a broad spectrum of different scenarios. Four meditations form the structure of the book and provide a mechanism for thinking about particular aspects of waterfront redevelopment. These meditations – "Connection to the Waterfront," "Remaking the Image of the City," "Port and City Relations" and lastly "New Waterfronts in Historic Cities" – form the general structure of the book. A comparison of two cities frames the context of each meditation. A series of reflections follow each city comparison. The book is structured to deal both with broad issues, that might be applicable to a variety of contexts, and with specific city descriptions which outlay the current state of waterfront development in these locations.

In "Connection to the Waterfront," Richard Marshall provides a comparison of waterfront developments in Vancouver and Sydney. The former industrial waterfront areas of many cities now exist as underutilized parcels, separated from the physical, social and economic activity of the rest of the city. In their reconsideration, these sites pose significant issues. How should that redevelopment occur? What is an appropriate form of development? What is an appropriate urban form? How are connections made between the older city and the water through these redevelopment efforts? Vancouver and Sydney provide two remarkable examples where these questions influence the production of new city space.

In Sydney, as in other cities, the connectivity of the physical fabric and the water suffered from the insertion of roads between city and harbor. This, combined with jurisdictional fragmentation, has tended to isolate major waterfront projects from the rest of the city. This is in spite of the fact that the image of the city is inextricably linked to its water. In defining the water as an urban amenity, Sydney faces such issues as the appropriateness of the waterside program and of connecting through, under or across large pieces of infrastructure.

In the 1980s, Vancouver developed the Central Area Plan to reinvent its inner city. Subsequently, the waterfront has changed from railway and industrial use to residential and recreational use. Today, stresses are emerging between integrated, mixed-use, fine-grained urban development and the needs of large-area programs. The need to accommodate large program uses, and to deal with the demands of the increased traffic and noise that they bring, is in conflict with the desire for human scaled waterfront precincts.

Vancouver and Sydney have strong relationships with their harbors. The balance of uses, in both of these contexts, acknowledges a strong desire for waterfront amenity. In comparison, these cities provide ways of thinking about appropriate use and access to urban waterfronts.

In his reflective essay, "Complexity on the Urban Waterfront," Rinio Bruttomesso explores the idea of complexity and program as a way to identify urban visions on the waterfront. Bruttomesso explores three operations of waterfront redevelopment – recomposition, regeneration, and recovery. At a time where present understandings of what makes a city are questionable, the waterfront offers remarkable opportunities to define and describe a contemporary view of life. Bruttomesso explores the application of program, and its ordering and articulation in light of this understanding of the contemporary condition. Bruttomesso argues that it is the co-presence of numerous activities on the waterfront that gives life to new pieces of city.

In the second theme, "Remaking the Image of the City," Richard Marshall deals with relationships between the renewal strategies in Bilbao and Shanghai and their river waterfronts. Marshall explores the relationship between the renewal in urban waterfronts and city-wide rethinking. Competitive advantage has become the catch-cry of the modern era. Competitive advantage is an essential aspect to many national, regional and local urban policy agendas. In a world of unprecedented technological change and the development of a truly integrated global economy, the competition to attract wealth, in physical and human terms, is even more crucial. A crucial aspect of these repositioning efforts is environmental, and urban regeneration and the most visible locations for this regeneration lie on the waterfront.

Cities will not succeed by ignoring the physical realm of the city. As cities shift from industrial to service economies, a major aspect of their success will be in the quality of their urban environments. It is here that the waterfront plays a critical role. Waterfronts are often the most degraded places in the city, being the sites of the former industries. Waterfronts are also highly visible locations in most cities. The image of the city can be remade here.

Bilbao and Shanghai are two examples of how the waterfront has become the stage for a new expression of city aspirations. These cities both have a long history of waterfront neglect. Bilbao represents a case study in how a waterfront can provide opportunities for the creation of a new identity, a new expression of what the city is and wants to be.

Shanghai, likewise, is a city in transition from an industrial foundation to one where issues of city quality are becoming critical.

Martin Millspaugh reflects on his twenty-five years of delivering water-front projects in "Waterfronts as Catalysts for City Renewal." The Baltimore Inner Harbor Redevelopment is an iconic waterfront project. It was the flagship for Baltimore's renaissance from being another part of the rust belt surrounding Washington, DC to becoming a major destination on the eastern seaboard of the United States. He outlines the essential aspects of his Baltimore experience, and explores the role of capital in waterfront development. The urban waterfront, as postcard view, has the ability to shape an image for a city, to add value to city economies, and create desirability. Millspaugh argues that the delivery system for these types of projects is critical. In the Baltimore case, the establishment of a private, single purpose, no stock corporation contracted to manage the development process was the key to Baltimore's ultimate success.

Alfonso Vegara elaborates on the role of waterfront redevelopment as a catalyst for new social relations in the city in "New Millennium Bilbao." Vegara describes the redevelopment process of Bilbao and focuses on the importance of the Nervión River. The Nervión River, once a physical and social barrier in the city, has become an axis of urban development for the entire city region.

Recent decades have witnessed substantial changes in port-city and city-port-region relationships. With changes in the nature of port operations and infrastructure, ports have been shifting to deepwater locations in order to maintain their competitive advantage. Such moves cause major changes in port and urban relations and influence the environments of coastal zones. Richard Marshall deals with the changing nature of this relationship in "Modern Ports and Historic Cities," through an examination of Genoa and Las Palmas de Gran Canaria.

The modern port has become a more complicated infrastructure. With changes in international transport, leading toward intermodalism and multimodalism, the port has lost its central position as focus of transportation and modal transfer. Instead, there are many such locations in the city-region. Ports must adapt to changing conditions and competition. The changing nature of port functions and the role of transportation have critical consequences for urban environments (Hoyle, 1996: 3). Historically the administrative functions of modern ports and cities have been completely separate. Zones of overlap have been the battleground of modern planning in many cities. Often ports fear that urban development, particularly waterfront housing, will influence and restrict essential port operations. Likewise, cities fear that an increase in port business will create more traffic and noise in residential areas.

"Modern Ports and Historic Cities" deals with the nature of those changes in two locations: Genoa and Las Palmas de Gran Canaria. These port cities provide two examples where these conflicts continue to influence the form of the city. Genoa is a case of enlightened relationships between the Port Authority and the Municipality. Las Palmas is somewhat more the norm. Both, however, shed light on the nature of this relationship and the importance of it in shaping the urban condition. Of particular importance to Marshall's investigation is the influence on the physical construction of the city and how the zone of overlap and conflict is managed.

The waterfront and port of Las Palmas de Gran Canaria, in Spain, epitomizes the transformation that is occurring with older port facilities. With changes in the nature of the port, there exist opportunities to create an alternative environment that allows for reconciliation with existing urban areas and a radical reshaping of the waterfront. Part of this reshaping is a matter of programmatic invention and economic incentives, while part is a matter of poetic imagination and the creation of a new urban architectural context. Las Palmas itself is neither a tourist haven nor a residential resort for the well-to-do, further adding to the relative vagueness of future waterfront development potentials.

Throughout history, Genoa has gone through alternative periods of great prosperity and profound crisis. After each crisis, the city has radically changed in terms of its economic structure and social organization. The world-wide restructuring of industry, the conversion of maritime transport modes, and the crisis in the system of state shareholdings in the industry represent a challenge for the city. The 1990s have produced the first results of this conversion with an increase in port traffic after years of decline, the realization of initiatives to reutilize industrial areas, and the positioning of Genoa as a tourist destination. The interface between port and city in Genoa is dynamic.

In "Port and City Relations: San Francisco and Boston" Anne Cook, Richard Marshall and Alden Raine reflect on the changing nature of the port and city relationship in the American context. Both Boston and San Francisco have always been port cities. The importance of the port in these cities in the eighteenth and nineteenth centuries led to the growth of Boston and San Francisco as major cities. Competition, obsolete infrastructure and the development of alternatives to sea transport eroded the place of the waterfront after the First World War in Boston and a little later in San Francisco. Since the early 1970s, significant efforts helped to secure the waterfront as an urban amenity in both of these locations. Boston is still coping with how to deal with its waterfront. San Francisco's relationship with its water edge dates to the California Gold Rush, a time of tremendous expansion for the San Francisco Bay. During the twentieth century, the waterfront became an industrial area of finger piers, railroad terminals, warehouses and a logistics center for the Pacific theater during the Second World War. Today, shipping and ship repair are located primarily south of China Basin and cruise ships, ferries, recreational boating and commercial maritime operations remain on the northern waterfront.

"Port and City Relations" deals with the relationship between Massport and the Boston Redevelopment Authority and reflects on the dynamics of port, city and community in the South Boston Waterfront. It reflects on the challenge of balancing primary port operations with community concerns by looking at the San Francisco Port Commission and the wider community. Of particular interest is the relationship that ports and cities have with their respective community interests. In San Francisco, relations between the Port and the residents were strained to the point where Proposition H was enacted and effectively blocked development proposals of the Port.

In the final meditation, "Waterfronts, Development and World Heritage

Cities," Richard Marshall deals with waterfront development in Amsterdam and Havana. The relationship of historic cities to new developments along the waterfront is of critical interest for older cities contemplating development of their waterfronts. Preservation of our built historical fabric is important to the creation of identity and the preservation of our character.

Amsterdam and Havana provide two cases where this balancing act between development and preservation along the waterfront occurs. Both deal with the pressure of real estate exploitation for capital gain over the desire to save the physical residue of history. These conflicting ideologies are at the heart of waterfront development in these cities. These contexts pose several questions. What is the appropriate form of this development? How does one protect the historic city from the consumptive nature of new capital development? How does one make relationships between the old and the new? How does new, often large, development situate itself amongst older, smaller, fabric?

Havana already is, and Amsterdam is to be, listed as a UNESCO World Heritage City. Amsterdam has been dealing with the redevelopment of its waterfront for some thirty years. The story of the Amsterdam waterfront is one of success and failure. Havana, in comparison, is just now beginning to deal with similar issues. One of the consequences of the victory of the Revolution on January 1, 1959 was the shift in priorities in Cuba from urban to rural development, sparing Havana the blight of commercial development common in other Caribbean cities. However, it has also meant that much of the basic upkeep of the city has not occurred. The result is that Havana is both a precious historic artifact and a city in desperate need of maintenance, repair and modernization.

The intricate inner city of Amsterdam, founded on the banks of the River Ij in the twelfth century, struggles to accommodate contemporary uses within its historic fabric. Because of this, Amsterdam is developing as a multi-polar city with different functions in different areas. The central aim for redevelopment of the River Ij was to strengthen the prominence of the inner city, and to re-establish a relationship between Amsterdam and the Ij.

Barry Shaw deals with the issue of balancing development with preservation interests in "History at the Water's Edge." Shaw describes the generational nature of waterfront development. He argues that the first generation of waterfront projects – the visionary projects such as in Boston and Baltimore – set the examples which others then followed. The second generation occurs when developers adopt and expand on these ideas. The third generation occurs when these redevelopment ideas become standard practice and a new generation of creative thinkers overhauls these standard models. Shaw then speculates on the nature of the fourth generation of waterfront development.

Alex Krieger, in "Reflections on the Boston Waterfront," explores how the image of what we know of the city today has been forged by extensive landfill operations occurring over three hundred years.

Krieger notes that "The impending reuse of an urban waterfront generally combines grand expectations with considerable self-reflection about the very nature of contemporary urbanism." And it is within this moment of self-reflection that planners and designers ask such questions as should planning for reuse support traditional maritime industries or promote new economies? Who should be attracted to this new zone – residents, new-comers or tourists? He asks, "Should commercial expansion be favored or multiple civic needs addressed, especially those which private initiative does not readily achieve? Should, for example, cities seek to profit from the scale of modern development attracted to reconnected waterfronts or restrict density while enlarging recreational space?"

Waterfronts not only provide us with remarkable opportunities for pro-jects but also for ways of thinking about contemporary space-making in the city. The nature and size of the waterfront efforts examined in this book are evidence of contemporary urbanization in process. They can be seen as partial visions of the contemporary city. In an age where central concerns for the city relate, on the one hand, to issues of urban sprawl, and on the other to the emptying of historic cores, the urban waterfront provides us with opportunities to consolidate the void, to define the edge and to create a new urban vision of ourselves. As Alex Krieger writes, it is "along its waterfront [that] the aura of a city resides and persists."

Bibliography

Breen, A. and Rigby, D. (1994) *Waterfronts: Cities Reclaim their Edge*, New York: McGraw-Hill.

Breen, A. and Rigby, D. (1996) *The New Waterfront: A Worldwide Urban Success Story*, New York: McGraw-Hill.

Brutomesso, R. (ed.) (1998) *Land–Water Intermodal Terminals*, Venice: Marsilio Editori.

Brutomesso, R. (ed.) (1999) "Aquapolis: the maturity of the waterfront," *International Centre Cities on Water* IV (3–4), September–December.

Brutomesso, R. (ed.) (1999) *Water and Historical Heritage*, Venice: Marsilio Editori.

Davey, P. (1999) "Public realm," *Architectural Review*, 206 (1229), July: 32–33.

Ellin, N. (1999) *Postmodern Urbanism*, New York: Princeton Architectural Press.

Goodman, David C. (1999) *European Cities and Technology: Industrial to Post-industrial Cities*, London: Routledge.

Hall, P. (1991) *Waterfronts: The New Urban Frontier*, Berkeley: University of California.

Hall, P. and Beaker, A. (1991) *Towards the Post-industrial City: A Symposium on Structural Change, Urban Problems, and Local Policies in the Regions of Frankfurt and San Francisco*, Working paper 543, Institute of Urban and Regional Development, University of California at Berkeley.

Hoyle, B. (1996) *Cityports, Coastal Zones, and Regional Change: Perspectives on Planning and Management*, Chichester and New York: Wiley.

Hoyle, B. and Pinder, D. (1981) *Cityport Industrialization and Regional Development: Spatial Analysis and Planning Strategies*, Oxford and New York: Pergamon Press.

Hoyle, B. and Pinder, D. (1988) *Revitalising the Waterfront: International Dimensions of Dockland Redevelopment*, London and New York: Belhaven Press.

Hudson, B. (1996) *Cities on the Shore: The Urban Littoral Frontier*, London and New York: Pinter.

Malone, P. (1996) *City, Capital and Water*, London and New York: Routledge.

Meyer, H. (1999) *City and Port: Urban Planning as a Cultural Venture in London, Barcelona, New York, and Rotterdam: Changing Relations between Public Urban Space and Large-scale Infrastructure*, Utrecht, Netherlands: International Books.

Morrison, F. (1991) "Sydney! Sydney!," *Urban Design Quarterly* 39: 3–5.

Rowe, P. (1997) *Civic Realism*, Cambridge, Mass: The MIT Press.

Savitch, H. V. (1988) *Post-industrial Cities: Politics and Planning in New York, Paris, and London*, Princeton, N.J.: Princeton University Press.

Schwarzer, M. (1998) "Ghostwards: the flight of capital from history," *Thresholds* 16 (Spring): 10–19.

PART II
CONNECTION TO THE WATERFRONT

2 Connection to the waterfront
Vancouver and Sydney

Richard Marshall

The nature of many former industrial waterfronts in the post-industrial city is problematic. Typically, these sites are underutilized parcels, separated from the physical, social and economic activity of the rest of the city. The reasons for this are well documented. These were the sites of industry and served their former functions extremely well. These were the sites where the Industrial Revolution was manifest, where the wealth of cities and nations was made. Today, these sites no longer serve these functions and, more often than not, they leave us with a tragic legacy of toxic contamination. In their reconsideration, these sites pose significant issues. Their legacy is that in many cities around the world there are now large parcels of land, often contaminated, waiting for redevelopment. How should that redevelopment occur? What is an appropriate form of development? What

2.1 Sydney Opera House.

is the relationship of waterfront sites to contemporary city making? How can these isolated parcels be reconfigured to make connections between older city centers and the water's edge?

Today we wonder how the planners and architects of yesterday could allow highways to be built along the waterfront and destroy these valuable city assets. Today we think of the waterfront as a urban amenity, a special place in the city. However, the waterfront as a site of amenity is a relatively recent phenomenon. Attitudes toward the waterfront have changed significantly over the last fifty years. The reasons should be obvious; waterfronts were the working areas of the city. As places of industry, they were dirty and messy and held little value in our collective conscience. They were places that were to be avoided at all costs.

Vancouver and Sydney are two waterfront cities that exemplify the changing nature of waterfront development. These cities continue to struggle with the problem of creating contemporary environments that are free from nuisance, overcrowding, noise, danger and pollution. They seek to answer the question of what is an appropriate level of amenity in areas that have suffered almost a century of neglect? Of critical concern in both redevelopment efforts is how to re-establish pedestrian networks through the city to the water's edge.

Over the last three decades, Vancouver has been steadily transforming its waterfront. For most of the previous one hundred years, the city's waterfront has been dominated by seaborne shipping facilities, railway yards, shipbuilding yards and lumber-based industry. Although there still exists some evidence of this industrial history, the city today is looked at as a model of post-industrial city-making. Vancouver's success is unique in a number of respects. It is a city that has been able to implement innovative high-quality, high-density developments along its inner city waterfront when most of the North American continent has been fleeing to the less dense suburban fringe. At a time when other inner cities have suffered from a lack of development, Vancouver has redeveloped its entire waterfront over the last twenty years.

In Sydney, the myth of the waterfront is somewhat different to its reality. Sydney is widely considered as a waterfront success story. In many publications, Sydney is presented as the "picture postcard waterfront city." However, although Sydney is situated in one of the world's most scenic harbors it provides relatively few opportunities to access the edge of the water. Connections between the city and the water are few. In many respects, Sydney operates as two distinct realms: the realm of the harbor and the realm of the city. These two realms only make contact with each other at a few select points. The harbor is a powerful realm that projects the image of the city, defines its identity and compensates for the "accidental" nature of the other, urban realm.

In comparison, Vancouver and Sydney provide two cases of cities struggling with difficult redevelopment contexts. Both cities provide lessons that others can learn from. Vancouver's efforts have a great deal to do with its progressive planning model. Also, that its waterfront, through either extreme far-sightedness or extreme good luck, avoided much of the urban infrastructure that other cities have been forced to deal with. Sydney is rather more the rule than the exception; its redevelopment efforts have suffered from political fragmentation and the fact of highways at the water's edge. What is interesting about these two conditions is the commitment to quality and the acknowledgement of the water as a resource for the city.

The Vancouver context

Since Expo'86, Vancouver has been carefully and strategically remaking itself. Its waterfront redevelopment efforts are the focus of considerable international interest. Other cities look to it as a model and seek to understand how it has been able to implement innovative high-quality, high-density housing, streetscapes and public spaces along its waterfront. Its location has allowed it to benefit from the explosive growth in Asia, which has led to a significant increase in population and, with it, the availability of capital for development. Despite being located on a small peninsula, the

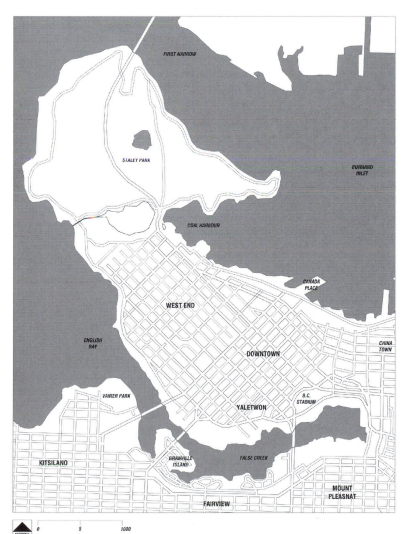

2.2 Map of Vancouver waterfront.

2.3 View of Vancouver City.

city provides numerous case studies for the redevelopment of former industrial space along the waterfront.

Vancouver sits on the southwest coast of British Columbia, surrounded by mountains and water. It lies at the mouth of the Fraser River Valley, bordered by the Coastal Mountains to the north and the Strait of Georgia to the west. The population of Vancouver is approaching two million people, which makes it the third largest city in Canada. The inner city and Stanley Park lie on a peninsula jutting into the strait, with the Burrard Inlet to the north and False Creek to the south. With a history of British colonial rule and Pacific Rim influences, Vancouver has become one of the major urban centers on the west coast of North America.

The city has always had a strong relationship with its harbor. It was chartered and explored by Europeans with the arrival of José Manuel Navarez in 1791 and Captain George Vancouver in 1792. Colonization was initially slow, based primarily on the terminus of continental trade and exploration routes, resource extraction and the advantages offered by its natural harbors. With the entrance of British Columbia into the Canadian Confederation in 1871, and the subsequent completion of the transcontinental railway in 1879, a period of major immigration and development began. Incorporated in 1886, the City of Vancouver suffered a terrible fire and was completely destroyed that same year. In its centennial year, Vancouver made its entrance onto the global stage by hosting the World's Fair, Expo'86. Since then, Vancouver has enjoyed continued growth spurred in large part to trans-Pacific migration and business connections.

Vancouver's dominant industry remains the production and distribution of raw materials – lumber, mining, fishing and shipping. Because of this, the city is one of the chief ports on the North American west coast, acting as the terminus for a number of major transcontinental rail lines. The city is a distribution point for products moving between North America and various ports in Asia. Vancouver's economy is expanding, with the growth of eco-tourism, the rise of communications, electronics, biotechnology and software development, and its growing motion picture industry. In fact, Vancouver is the third largest production site for motion pictures in North America after Los Angeles and New York. The Alaskan cruise industry has made Vancouver its primary embarkation point, bringing major revenues and large numbers of tourists to the city during the summer cruise season.

The Sydney context

Sydney shares some striking similarities with Vancouver. Both are former British colonies with extensive networks to the Pacific Rim. Sydney was founded in 1788, when the first fleet arrived from England to establish the penal colony of New South Wales under the direction of Captain Arthur Phillip. The city takes its name from Thomas Townsend, the first Viscount Sydney, who was Secretary of State for the British colonies at the time. Convict transportation from England to New South Wales continued until 1840.

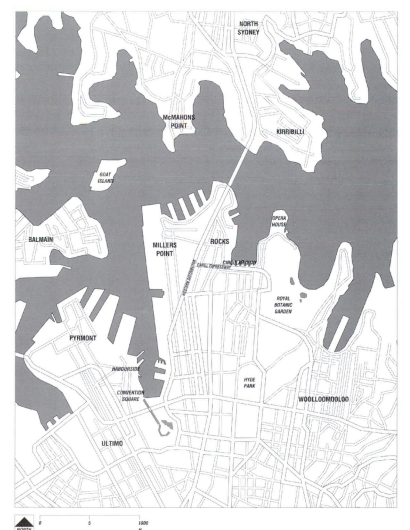

2.4 Map of Sydney waterfront.

Sydney, like Vancouver, has always had a strong relationship with its harbor. Its two famous icons, the Harbour Bridge and the Opera House, are harbor structures and constitute the essence of the city's self-image. From the earliest settlement, the city became an active seaport with commercial contact to the Pacific islands, India, China, South Africa and the Americas.

Sydney is one of the largest cities in the world in terms of area. The metropolitan area of Sydney covers some 1,600 square kilometers (620 sq. miles), equal to London and more than double the size of New York. The City of Sydney, which is the central business core of the city, is a tight and relatively small city center. The form of the city center reflects its harbor setting. Similarly to Vancouver, the City of Sydney is bound on three sides by water and is located on a narrow, intensely developed peninsula. The city displays a pre-industrial street pattern of narrow crooked streets.

Sydney is the major financial and business center of Australia and a significant node in the Asia-Pacific Region. Within the City of Sydney, some 200,000 people work in 10.5 million square feet of floor space. This population generates nearly half a million traffic movements every day. From 1991 to 1999, a period characterized by inner city desertions, especially in the United States, the number of inner city residents in Sydney more than trebled, from 7,300 to 24,000. The result of this growth, as one might imagine, is that all space in the City of Sydney is heavily contested.

Given that the harbor is the defining element in the image of the city, it is remarkable that the desirability of the water's edge, as a place to live and work, is a recent phenomenon. For much of the city's history, its downtown port, located in Sydney Cove, was regarded as an unsavory part of the city. Circular Quay was a working part of the city, and living conditions in the now fashionable Rocks area were so poor as to support an outbreak of the bubonic plague as late as 1900. Reflecting the lack of appreciation the water held for early Sydney residents, the Town Hall and the commercial center of the city were established away from the water's edge, on higher ground. It was only in the 1950s, with the removal of the city's statutory 150-foot height limit, that the waterfront became an attractive commercial location.

The Vancouver waterfront

Growth management initiatives have been in place in Vancouver's metropolitan area since the 1960s. One of the earliest was the Agricultural Land Reserve, adopted to preserve Fraser Valley farmland. In a province with mountainous terrain, the protection of flat agricultural land is of prime importance. More recently, the Liveable Region Strategy has directed new growth into a network of nine regional town centers of higher densities and mixed uses. Downtown Vancouver is the primary center of the Strategy.

Vancouver has become a model for other cities, not only as a result of its waterfront redevelopment but also in terms of its planning process. The development process in Vancouver comprises several stages. These include the creation of a policy statement to guide development planning, the cre-

2.5 View toward First Narrows with Canada Place in the foreground.

ation of an official development plan and, finally, the rezoning of a site to permit development in accordance with the established policies. This process of "progressive planning" is based upon a highly discretionary regulatory framework, which emphasizes guidance and incentives over hard regulations. Progressive planning is an exhaustive process of collaboration between the public and private sectors and the community. All three are engaged in constant dialogue throughout the course of a development. The public and private sectors join forces for the design exercise, policy is determined by politicians, development approvals are granted by appointed officials, and, for the most part, City decisions are final with appeals being rare. The result is that the rezoning process seldom stalls, because the community has been engaged thoroughly in the process.

Vancouver's waterfront began to change in the 1970s. The first waterfront redevelopment was Southeast False Creek. This project now includes approximately 2,000 residential units, 90,000 square feet of commercial space and 35 acres of park. Around the same time, Granville Island was redeveloped into a public space. Medium-density, ground-oriented, clustered developments, including new housing, parkland and a seawall pathway followed and started to reposition activity in the city. During this time, the provincial government assembled and cleared industrial land along the North Shore of False Creek for Expo'86. BC Place, a large indoor football stadium, was the first project built on these lands. The second

2.6 Reconstituted waterfront in Vancouver.

2.7 Vancouver city model: view toward False Creek.

large facility, also constructed for Expo'86, was Canada Place, a convention facility located on a pier in the Burrard Inlet.

The renaissance of the Vancouver waterfront derives from a specific period in the history of the city, with implementation of the regional growth strategy going into full gear after Expo'86. The entire Expo site, comprising some 204 acres, except for BC Stadium, was sold to a consortium of international developers under the name of Concord Pacific. The sale was conditional upon approval by the city of a development plan that conferred a certain amount of floor space and specified a package of public benefits. In addition to basic infrastructure, this package included 17 hectares of parkland, a continuous walking and bike system, a community center, childcare and school sites, a public art program, and a 20 percent social housing requirement. The project includes 8,500 residential units and 2.6 million square feet of commercial space. The development plan was devised under a cooperative planning model, between the city, the province, the developers, their consultants, and the public. Since the initial sale of land, some portions of the site have been sold to other developers who have generally continued to implement the plan. The False Creek North plan calls for 10,000 housing units and 42 acres of parkland to be constructed over twenty years. One-third of the housing and two-thirds of the park space have now been built with another 1,000 units of housing to be constructed in the east end of the inlet.

2.8 High-rise housing on the Vancouver waterfront.

In 1991, the City of Vancouver adopted the "Central Area Plan" to reinvent its inner city. In the North American context, the Central Area Plan is a revolutionary document. It advocates very intensive, high-density, inner city development with an emphasis on housing. Ultimately it is a plan that promotes a specific urban lifestyle – one that is a radical departure from the suburban ideal. It advocates inner city living, aims at reducing the reliance on the motor car, and re-establishes the idea of community in an urban setting. In many respects, this plan is the antithesis of half a century of un-city making on the North American continent. It also calls for large-scale changes in land use, particularly on the waterfront, from industrial and railway use to residential and recreational use.

A massive redevelopment project is also taking shape on the former industrial and railway lands in Coal Harbor on the Burrard Inlet. The site was owned by Canadian Pacific Railway who transferred the ownership to Marathon Realty in 1990. A development plan was devised conditional upon approval of certain requirements that include a specific package of public benefits, similar to False Creek North. This package includes 12 acres of parkland, a continuous waterfront walking and bike system, a community center, childcare facilities, a public art program, an arts center, and a 20 percent social housing requirement. Sites are now being sold for development. Adjacent to the Marathon site is Bayshore Gardens, owned by Japanese developers Aoki, which has followed in a similar manner.

The East Shore of False Creek was also used for Expo'86, but remained the property of a private industrial company. After Expo'86, the site was rezoned for residential use and sold to Bosa Developments, a local developer, who implemented a comprehensive plan known as City Gate. The project comprises 14 acres, 1,500 residential units and 370,000 square feet of commercial space.

Connection between the new waterfront residential areas and the older downtown is facilitated by the extension of existing city streets and by infill developments designed to mesh the older downtown to the recreated water's edge. With these developments, 7,500 housing units have been added to the inner city in the past decade and another 16,000 are planned. The form of this connective tissue has been middle to high-rise towers rising out of residential or retail podiums. This strategy has been successful in meeting the regional growth objectives for the city, which include raising the jobs–housing ratio, creating social and cultural diversity, encouraging transit use, and supporting a more environmentally sustainable city.

The Southeast Shore of False Creek is the last piece of industrial waterfront to be planned for residential use. The City of Vancouver owns the site and in addition to meeting the regional objectives of concentrated, mixed-use growth, this project aims to be a model for sustainable development in a high-density urban context. The project covers 80 acres of land and allows for some 5,000 residential units with very limited commercial space. Explicit targets for sustainability have been set, a policy framework has been completed, and specific community development planning is now underway. In this case, sustainable urban development refers to a neighborhood which "is integrated with its urban context while protecting and enhancing the social and economic health of its community as well as

2.9 Urban grid of Vancouver.

the health of local and global ecosystems." Where other projects may make similar claims regarding the social and economic aspects of sustainability, Southeast False Creek is remarkable for its attempt to develop an ecologically sustainable urban development. Southeast False Creek's sustainability goals include maximizing the diversion of all wastes from disposal, minimizing the need for travel outside of the project for basic amenities, providing alternatives for single occupancy vehicle travel outside the neighborhood, reducing non-renewable energy consumption, minimizing harmful emissions, minimizing water pollution, and maximizing the restoration of aquatic environments.

A strong citizens' lobby advocating the site for public parkland has complicated civic approvals for this project. The plan is now proceeding, with two-thirds of the site designated as park space. On the remaining site, stakeholders envision 3,000 medium-density, ground-oriented, residential units. The City is expected to carry the property through to new zoning then sell off areas slated for redevelopment.

While the City restructuring continues rapidly in the inner city waterfronts, stresses are beginning to emerge from the accommodation of major facilities. These include facilities constructed for Expo'86, including Canada Place, BC Place Stadium, Plaza of the Nations Entertainment Center, and Science World. Post-Expo facilities include General Motors

2.10 View toward BC Place, Vancouver.

Place, a hockey/basketball arena, and a new central library. Current projects in planning include an expansion of the convention center and a cruise ship terminal on the downtown waterfront, as well as a new arts center. Pressure is mounting on the few available large waterfront sites to accommodate these facilities. Further, such facilities impact their immediate contexts through increased traffic and noise levels and the rendering of areas out of scale with the more integrated, mixed-use, fine-grained urban development of the surrounding waterfront. These considerations have led to current efforts to manage the impact of these large projects. These include containing major-facility site assignments, facilitating neighborhood development before displacement can occur, arranging tight development juxtapositions to moderate issues of scale, and overlaying new urban design solutions on previously built sites to achieve ambience, accessibility, and a mix of uses.

The Sydney waterfront

With its cooperative planning model, Vancouver is a model of enlightened city planning. Sydney, in comparison, is a case where the city's development process has been complicated and at times compromised by jurisdictional fragmentation. For many years, a proliferation of consent bodies, competing for the control of Sydney's relatively small central city area, have encouraged a feudal mindset on the part of many city planners and authorities. This has led to conditions where major city redevelopments have become unnecessarily confined within artificial boundaries, resulting

in the squandering of opportunities to integrate new pieces of city with the existing fabric. Even today, territorial disputes between the state and local governments continue to compromise long-term planning efforts in the city.

Sydney describes itself as an accidental city. Sydney's physical history has been shaped by commercial and political motives above any sense of a public realm (City Spaces, 1999 "City Spaces – Sydney's potential"). However, there is a growing sense that the public realm needs to be a priority. Documents such as the "Central Sydney Local Environment Plan" of 1996 and "City Spaces" of 1999 make a series of long-term proposals for the city's public realm and aim for design excellence in the creation of urban places.

Development attitudes have changed significantly over the past three decades. The 1960s produced a series of large-scale redevelopment projects, analogous to many urban renewal projects in the United States. The redevelopment of Woolloomooloo, The Rocks, Victoria Street and the demolitions that occurred in Redfern are examples. The 1980s produced the "Festival Market" model, most clearly found at Darling Harbour, on the western edge of the city center.

Darling Harbour is often cited as a waterfront success story. Indeed the project has been successful in many respects; visitor numbers, for example, are in the order of fifteen million people *The New Waterfront: A worldwide urban success story* (Breen and Rigby, 1996). However, when viewed within the wider urban context, it is an example of a major project failing to integrate itself into the fabric of the city. Conceived in the early 1980s, as one of a number of bicentennial projects for 1988, Darling Harbour is a 134-acre harbor redevelopment adjacent to the central business district of Sydney. The project was one of several around the world developed on the Baltimore Harborside model and was made possible by State Government ownership of most of the land. Developed with a mix of public and private sector funding, the intention was to make a "place for people" by converting an obsolete railway yard, crossed by overhead motorways, into a center for cultural, educational and recreational activity.

Given the need to develop the project for Sydney's bicentennial in 1988, a development corporation was established to hasten the construction of the project. The Darling Harbour Authority, established to facilitate this goal, was both the landowner and consent authority for the development. To fast-track the development schedule, the Authority was granted exemption from development control legislation involving numerous State and Local Government agencies.

The project includes the Sydney Convention, Entertainment and Exhibition Centers, museums including the Australian Maritime Museum, theaters, the Harbourside Shopping Center, the Chinese Garden, the Sydney Aquarium, Cockle Bay Restaurant and entertainment complex and a wide range of bars, hotels and restaurants. The limited success of the project is due to its capacity to accommodate large footprint facilities within close proximity to the center of the city. One wonders why such facilities need to be all in one place; nevertheless the project was able to supply needed large indoor venues. Further, success is gained through the provision of much-needed public open space adjacent to the waterfront in close proximity to a variety of facilities and other adjacent developments, high-density housing and urban parks.

2.12 View from Sydney's Darling Harbour toward city.

However, despite these measures of success, there are lessons to be learned from Darling Harbour. Even now, despite its proximity, the project remains relatively isolated from the rest of the city. The Western Distributor, which encircles and cuts through the site, is a major contributor to this isolation. The project's separation is reinforced both by the project's underlying conception as a bounded campus development, and by its administrative isolation from the city. Because of the fact that the Authority was granted exemption from development controls, it did not communicate well with other agencies in the city. This, rather inevitably, meant that no attempt was made to integrate the development into the fabric of the city – for example, to extend existing roads into the development site or to establish unified and consistent development controls. The result of this inward-looking development is that many of Darling Harbour's larger facilities, including the exhibition and convention buildings, hotels and the Star City Casino complex, form a formidable wall around the site, turning their backs to the rest of the city.

The project's zoning has also played a part in the separation of the project from the city. The project's original leisure theme included retail and entertainment activities of many kinds, but no residential or commercial space. The reliance of retail to facilitate public space in the city has proven suspect in many cities around the world. The incorporation of singular large box retail was from the start problematic in many ways. The lack of resident population meant that Darling Harbour's retail component was forced to rely solely on visitors. This not only means that the project dies at night, but also that the retailers in the Harbourside complex have struggled. With the increasing redevelopment of Pyrmont, some of this will be alleviated. In many respects, Darling Harbour's "big box" program is a suburban development transplanted into the city. Although such trans-urban migration has occurred in other locations as well, the lesson to be learnt from this project is that such programs need to be integrated into the fabric of the host city. Connections to the host city are critical to the success of such projects. At Darling Harbour these connections are now under review.

A different paradigm for Darling Harbour may have proven more successful. Speaking purely speculatively, one wonders whether Darling Harbour might not have been better served with public and cultural facilities with associated retail development. The same amount of retail could have been incorporated into the project but would have been scattered across the 134-acre site, alleviating some of the noticeable "dead zones" in the development.

The popularity of inner city living in Sydney has led to the resurgence of many inner city neighborhoods in close proximity to the city center. Pyrmont and Ultimo, adjacent to Darling Harbour, are two of the peripheral neighborhoods, along with Miller's Point and Chinatown, where most of the city's nearly 25,000 resident population lives. The last remaining opportunity for any large-scale redevelopment adjacent to the central business district is the container wharf in an area known as the Western Wharves (Wharves 6–8), located on the eastern shore of Darling Harbour.

The larger part of Sydney's working port facility has already moved south to Botany Bay. It is therefore likely that, at some time in the future,

2.13 View toward Circular Quay from McMahons Point, Sydney.

the remaining port facilities will vacate Wharves 6–8. This constitutes a major opportunity to add another major residential project to the Sydney waterfront. The project, entitled "The West Village," involves a new mixed residential and parkland development on the city's western fringe. Centered on a waterfront square, the development would include residential support facilities such as shops and schools as well as small-scale office activities, recreational facilities and a major waterfront park. The West Village will be accessible via a proposed new heavy rail station near Wynard, extra ferry services, and an additional light rail station. It provides a rare opportunity in Sydney to expand public access to the harbor foreshore and improve the quality of inner city streets by the relocation of container truck traffic.

Connection in the city is hampered most conspicuously by roadways constructed in the 1950s and 1960s. Ironically, by the time the waterfront was recognized as a valuable commodity, Sydney had alienated its prime waterfront strip, along Circular Quay, with the erection of an elevated road and railway. This structure, known as the Cahill Expressway, provides access to the Harbour Bridge, enabling Sydney's central business district to be linked to the other side of the harbor on the North Shore.

Circular Quay is the symbolic gateway to both the city of Sydney and to Australia. It is here that Captain Phillip and the first fleet landed to establish the penal colony of New South Wales. Today it is flanked by both the Opera House and the Harbour Bridge. Despite the symbolism and geography of the Quay, the public space along Alfred Street is constricted and separated from the water by the Cahill Expressway. The City of Sydney has long supported the idea of demolishing the Expressway and reconnecting the city to the water. The idea would involve considerable restructuring to the transportation network of the city. The Boston Central Artery project is one example of a like project. The aim is to liberate Circular Quay from the shadow of the Expressway and reconnect the city with the water edge at the Quay.

The removal of the roadway structure would enable the frontage between Alfred Street and the Quay itself to be transformed into an open space on a scale seldom seen in Sydney. Sydney has some grand urban parks, notably Hyde Park; however, besides Martin Place and the Pitt Street Mall, Sydney has few urban plazas. It should be noted, however, that there are new squares and parks being made in the city, driven by the development rush of the Olympics – notably, Chifley Square, Railway Square, and Cook and Phillip Park. The Circular Quay proposal would extend the newly refurbished Customs Square, creating a major ceremonial space in the city, and extend the potential of the Opera House, the Museum of Contemporary Art, the art cinemas in the New East Circular Quay building, and various art and craft galleries within the Customs House. In addition, the new Cinamatheque and Museum of Australian Architecture within the Museum of Contemporary Art will substantially reinforce this idea. In some respects the idea for a Cultural Quay would serve Sydney in the same way that the South Bank serves London.

2.14 Customs House Square, Sydney.

The extension of the Cultural Quay will include the controversial East Circular Quay development. This site, on the promontory leading out to the Sydney Opera House, was home to the warehouses of the wool trade for much of the nineteenth century. During the waterfront boom of the 1950s and 1960s, the warehouses were replaced with some of Sydney's first curtain wall office buildings, including Unilever House, designed by Harry Seidler in 1957. Since the designation of Bennelong Point as the site for the Opera House, development on East Circular Quay has been a contentious issue. Jorn Utzon's winning design for the Opera House in 1962 was accompanied by drawings of a 15-story wall of office development along the East Circular Quay site. Utzon saw this as a way to frame the setting of the Opera House. The recent history of the site continues the debate and is evidence that not everyone shares Utzon's views.

In 1984, a government-controlled consent body was established to oversee the future of East Circular Quay. In 1992, the City of Sydney held a public ideas competition, which attracted some 200 submissions. Indicating the polarity of the views for the site, submissions ranged from low-scale parks to projects that maximized the allowable building density. The Lord Mayor of Sydney, Frank Sartor, established a panel of experts to assess the competition ideas, and a set of design guidelines was developed for the site. These guidelines mandated a low, horizontal development, which took account of view corridors across the Quay and encouraged public cultural uses at the ground level. They also proposed a six-meter-wide colonnade along the entire length of the building that would lead people from the Quay to the Opera House.

Acting on legal advice that there were existing consents on the five parcels which would allow for higher developments than allowed in the design guidelines, the City Council closed the existing roadway that services these parcels. Restricting access would ensure a lower height development and improve pedestrian uses at the ground floor. Meanwhile, the site's new owners, CML, had demolished several of the existing buildings, thereby exposing the empty site to public view, and reinstating the lost character of nineteenth-century vistas. This opened a new view to the Opera House from Circular Quay and an attachment to the idea of keeping the site "open" developed. The "no development" option could only occur through government intervention. However, no government was prepared to purchase the site.

In much the same way as Darling Harbour, Circular Quay has suffered a proliferation of consent and decision-making bodies. These include the City of Sydney, the Central Sydney Planning Committee, the State Minister for Planning, the Maritime Services Board, the Land and Environment Court, etc. In recognition of these inefficiencies, the Sydney Harbour Foreshores Authority was formed in February of 1999, amalgamating the functions of the City West Development Corporation, the Sydney Cove Authority and the Darling Harbour Authority (in January 2001). An AUS$22 million upgrade of the Quay and its ferry wharves is currently underway, under the auspices of the new authority.

For some time now advocates have promoted the idea of a waterfront promenade in Sydney. The existing walkway between the Opera House and Macquarie's Point at Farm Cove is extremely popular with both locals and visitors. The City of Sydney is currently promoting the development of a nine-mile waterfront promenade from Glebe to Garden Island. The promenade would take in Blackwattle Bay, Darling Harbour, Cockle Bay, Walsh Bay, Circular Quay, Sydney Cove, Farm Cove and Woolloomooloo Bay. Given the tremendous potential of Sydney Harbour, the promenade would be one of the most extraordinary waterfront promenades in the world.

Conclusion

We live in a cynical world and so it is not surprising that Vancouver's success attracts some level of skepticism. What are we not being told? Where are the hidden issues? However, Vancouver is a very strange place. Strange in the sense that where one's experience in other cities is of partial or fragmentary achievements, Vancouver appears to be a comprehensive success. A significant degree of that success can be attributed to some far-reaching decisions made in the 1960s. Most incredible, from a North American perspective, are the adoption of the Agricultural Land Reserve, an early growth control initiative, and the decision not to develop a freeway system. Instead, an arterial system of major roads allows for an array of movement in the city. In Vancouver, traffic congestion is looked upon in a positive light, and is intended to promote both alternative modes of transport and the demand for inner city living. Experience in other parts of the world, and especially in the United States, would suggest that Vancouver was doomed to failure. This same experience would suggest that free-flowing traffic is an essential aspect of a city's competitive advantage. Vancouver's success, on the contrary, proves this experience wrong. For cities such as Shanghai, who are just now constructing their expressway system, Vancouver proves that conventional wisdom is not always right and the possibility for success of another approach.

These two decisions have had a tremendous influence on Vancouver's subsequent waterfront redevelopment efforts. Together they promote an extremely high density, of which there are few contemporary North American models. The decision not to build freeways has meant that Vancouver, in an incredibly rare situation, has not had to deal with the implications of infrastructure along the water's edge. There are no expressways in Vancouver to take down because none were built in the first place. This means that Vancouver has been able to extend its existing road system, open space network, building typologies, materials and general urban morphology from the city, seamlessly into the new urban realm along the waterfront.

In these terms, Sydney is more typical and, taking nothing away from Vancouver, its successes are more hard gained. Sydney is a mythical city; its identity and consciousness are wholly determined by its harbor. The logo for the city is even an anchor! However, Sydney made all of the usual decisions, all the usual "mistakes," which resulted in expressways separating the city from the water's edge.

Sydney operates as two realms. One realm is the harbor and the other realm is the city. The harbor exists with a kind of protective wrapping

2.15 New housing in Vancouver, showing relationship of tower to residential podium.

around it, only penetrated at limited points. When one is in the city there is a constant awareness of the water – not in terms of an extension of the city but rather as some other place. There is a definite line of demarcation between the two. Even when sites become available for redevelopment along the harbor, such as Darling Harbour, in some strange way, both physically and jurisdictionally, the projects belong to the realm of the harbor and not to the city. Physically the project is isolated from the city by expressways. Jurisdictionally, the project was isolated by the city with the incorporation of the Darling Harbour Redevelopment Authority. Vancouver's projects, by comparison, have the absence of separating infrastructure and have resisted the establishment of "third agencies." The difference between Sydney and Vancouver can be described in terms of their attitudes toward waterfront development. In Sydney, the attitude is

2.16 View toward Sydney Harbour Bridge from Cremorne.

based on a project mentality, with parts of the waterfront considered separately in isolation from the city and from each other. In Vancouver, the waterfront is seen as an extension of the city and although it is developed project by project there exists clarity of thinking as to the whole.

For Sydney to reconnect with its water, more dramatic interventions will be necessary. Often discussions of urban design in Sydney describe expressways as major planning "mistakes." Whether they are mistakes or simply regrets is debatable. A mistake implies a slip of a pen or an act unintended. If the political parties in Sydney were committed to the quality of the physical realm of the city then the continuation of such "mistakes" would not occur. The continuation of the Eastern Distributor through the heart of Woolloomooloo, completed only recently, suggests that Sydney lacks the political will to define its urban presence.

In comparing Vancouver to Sydney, a critical difference needs to be articulated. This difference involves the political administration of the spaces in the city. Vancouver follows a typical North American model. The City is responsible for the development of the city. In Vancouver, as we have already discussed, development occurs with the public and private sectors joining forces for the design exercise, policy is determined by city politicians, and development approvals are granted by city-appointed officials. In Sydney, by comparison, the territory of the city is highly contested. This contest involves the State Government of New South Wales and the City of Sydney. Both lay claim to the space of the city in different ways and it is this lack of demarcation that lies at the heart of Sydney's schizophrenic urban development.

The State Government is very powerful in Sydney. The City and the Lord Mayor, in comparison, unlike the city governments and Mayors in North America, are relatively unempowered. The current urban renaissance in Sydney is remarkable when one realizes the relative weakness of the

2.17 View toward Garden Island from McMahons Point, Sydney.

jurisdictional control invested in the local government. Three reasons can be attributed to Sydney's current success – the single-minded determination and political skill of the Lord Mayor, Frank Sartor, the influx of money generated by the Sydney Olympics, and the fact that the State Government did not interfere. Real and long-term change in attitudes toward the physical realm of the city, however, will only be addressed if the State Government of New South Wales elevates planning as a primary undertaking. The Ministry for Planning is a minor portfolio in State politics. Only when planning is taken seriously in Sydney will the city achieve the potential that its remarkable harbor setting demands.

The issue for Sydney is whether it is ready to deal with its own sense of self. Is the city ready to make a statement about what type of place it should be? Is it ready to address the imbalance of the myth and reality of its waterfront? Is it ready to accept the potential of the waterfront to define its own vision of itself?

This chapter is based in large part upon case material prepared by the City of Vancouver and the City of Sydney, and on presentations by Vancouver City Councillor Lyn Kennedy, by Larry Beasely, Head of Planning for the City of Vancouver, and by the Lord Mayor of Sydney Frank Sartor at the Waterfronts in Post Industrial Cities Conference, 7–9 October, 1999, Harvard Design School, Cambridge, Massachusetts.

3 Complexity on the urban waterfront

Rinio Bruttomesso

The twentieth century has come to a close and we are left with an emblematic image of the end-of-the-century "city" which is difficult to connect with the one that opened this historic period in terms of continuity and development. The oldest parts have, of course, been conserved and almost always mark an identity, which has been maintained not only over the last hundred years but in some cases over the centuries. Without a doubt, some urban structures, such as the ports, are still recognizable, both because they have not shifted from their original positions and because they have maintained the profile and shape of places that are easily identified. Moreover, many pieces of infrastructure, such as certain roads or railway stations with their masses of rails, are still in place and highlight the lines of access to large urban conurbations, forming a sort of "framework" of the territory, often a leftover from the late nineteenth century.

The gradual process of growth of the nineteenth-century city came to an end with the urban extension which took place over the last century. This expansion led to the breakdown of the "forma urbis," determined in many European cities, for example, by the fragmentation of the defense apparatus which had "held in" and shaped the urban growth for centuries, both inside as well as outside the band of walls. However, even more surprising was the decline of the "industrial city," which took place in the second half of this century and was often both rapid and vast in scale, greatly modifying the image and structure of the twentieth-century city. These cities are in fact now defined as "post-industrial," a reality successive to the phase characterized by the growth of vast factories and imposing industrial complexes. The consequences of this passage are clear and weighty: firstly obsolescence, then the abandonment of vast industrial areas, buildings deserted, productive plants closed, with the relative problems of deterioration of both a physical and social nature of relevant portions of the urban fabric.

Many cities have reacted to this state of affairs with programs of regeneration and revitalization of the run-down areas, demonstrating that they have understood that the "post-industrial" phase cannot only be experienced through initiatives aimed at limiting the damage of the conclusion of a long and decisive era – namely, the growth of industry. Instead, they realize that sustaining this solution for continuity must be interpreted in a positive sense, as an opportunity for re-launching the urban economy, for trying out new objectives and new challenges. The story of the waterfront is thus to be found in this framework, this context of events and intentions, and I therefore feel that the waterfront should be interpreted as an essential paradigm of the post-industrial city.

The waterfront as an unusual outcome of the post-industrial city

While the vast abandoned industrial areas are the most visible and concrete testimony of the effects of an era that is coming to an end, we must remember that another, equally obvious, emblem of this transition are the events of the port areas which, convulsed by the revolution in maritime transport with the introduction of containers, have radically altered their set-ups: the ports have "freed" the parts more closely tied to the urban fabric, and have acquired new spaces, more peripheral and accessible from the hinterland. Many waterfront zones are or have been port zones, and interesting and obvious features can still be seen. Thus the end of the process of industrial growth, or rather its new course, is mainly characterized by a lack of need to use new areas (a difficult thing in any case in territory that is all but urbanized), but instead to exploit spaces and equipment that date back to the first industrial period: the main theme becomes that of recovering this heritage, affording it increased weight in policies of urban development as a resource to be upgraded rather than as an imposing and cumbersome inheritance of the past. In this sense re-launching the waterfront is one of the most significant chapters in these policies, as this urban zone, in direct contact with the water, has the same objectives as the old and abandoned industrial areas redesigned by the city; namely, the same three guidelines: "recomposition," "regeneration" and "recovery."

The first – "recomposition" – means that those in charge of the waterfront projects concentrate above all on giving a common unitary sense to the different parts – both physical and functional – which make up the areas (for example there are different sectors – often isolated from each other and non-communicative – that constitute the port areas in the very heart of the city, with spaces for commercial activities and storage completely separate from those destined for passengers). Therefore, the first clear outcome of these operations is the work of "re-joining" these parts and activating a new "character," one that can keep the different elements together while also furnishing an unusual and attractive image for future users.

"Regeneration" could also be seen as central to waterfront work, as it entails re-examining and revitalizing urban zones that are of a considerable size and often located a short distance from the city center. Whether these urban zones be former port areas or used for other purposes, whether the reused areas be empty or devoid of function, there can be no doubt concerning the strategic importance of this upgrading. The outcome is reintroduction into "urban play," with an increase in value, a considerable stock

3.1 Along the boardwalk at Pierhead on the Victoria and Alfred waterfront in Cape Town.

of areas assigning them conspicuous importance, as is often intended, through the re-launch of the waterfront, thus redefining the role and image of the entire city (from this point of view, the experience of Barcelona during the 1990s is of great importance and can be seen as exemplary).

Lastly, with the "recovery" projects for individual buildings or groups of structures, intervention on the waterfront has taken on further importance: that of the choice and introduction of new activities in abandoned or depressed zones, through the restructuring and restoration of buildings, often of great historic and architectural importance, which are significant examples of industrial archaeology. From this viewpoint, the context of the waterfront has, for many countries and cities, acted as a remarkable laboratory for intervention in existing areas, presenting projects that cover the full range of recovery possibilities: namely, moving from strict respect for the building (both in terms of the exterior appearance as well as the substantial conservation of the distribution of internal space) to more radical and consistent operations on the complex structure.

Industrial areas, and port zones on the "historic" waterfront, are the terrain, though not exclusively, for the application of the important and unusual urban renewal which characterizes the post-industrial city at the end of the twentieth century. The objective is often very ambitious as it aims not only to re-acquire strategically placed obsolete or abandoned zones but also to define a new "urban quality," to propose new "additions" that can offer higher living standards and which have the difficult and definitive function of helping re-launch the image and the role of the city on both a national and international scale.

In Europe in particular, where the process of industrialization and consolidation of port structures commenced earlier than elsewhere, it is already possible to identify many examples of this strategy, which saw the waterfront as a leading force in the future of the development of the city: in the United Kingdom (Liverpool, Glasgow, Cardiff), in France (Le Havre, Dunkerque, St Nazaire), in Germany (Hamburg, Bremen, Kiel), in Spain (Valencia, Malaga, Cadiz), in Italy (Genoa, Venice, Naples, Trieste) – to cite

3.2 View toward the Utopia Pavilion at the Lisbon Expo'98 site.

but a few examples and leaving aside the well-known cases of the London Docklands or Port Vell in Barcelona. It is a phenomenon which is already observable and which has recurrent features (though with several variations), together with unusual features, linked to the individual sites and local traditions. However, there is no doubt that this strategy was conceived, promoted, became popular and was consolidated on the North American continent – in the United States in particular – and became a "model" that was successively exported to the rest of the world from Europe to Japan and Australia. This was the first model of regeneration for urban-port waterfront areas entailing the conception of the renewal of the waterfront zone. The celebrated cases of Baltimore and Boston both enclosed the seeds of a new operation, which will certainly take on specific and distinctive tones from time to time and give rise to a vast range of outcomes; twenty-five years on the Baltimore and Boston cases are akin to a sort of "big bang" in waterfront redevelopment, a start – for many cities – of a new and powerful phase of urban reorganization.

The waterfront, a paradigm of urban complexity

On observing the main waterfront projects in detail, it is clear that one of the essential elements is the co-presence of numerous activities which, combined in different percentages depending on the cases, give life to new "pieces" of city, sometimes marked by an interesting feature entailing complexity. Complexity is a quality that distinguishes the more complete, articulated urban organisms. It is often the outcome of long processes involving successive historic phases and projects implemented in these phases; from this viewpoint, the complexity of the city is a product of intelligent and continuous work of construction, often over many centuries. However, complexity can also be the result of a single project, with different shades of importance, over the span of a matter of years – the result of a partial operation from one "sector" rather than a "general" planning act.

Careful examination reveals that the contemporary city often exhibits different qualities over different periods, in terms of construction: at times initiatives based on run-of-the-mill simplicity and an embarrassing poverty of intent are encountered (in the construction of certain residential districts, for instance, not to mention several zones destined for business activities); at other times individual buildings or urban zones (even of modest dimensions) offer a wealth of stimuli comparable to those typical of historical or more consolidated urban fabrics. Waterfront work has not escaped this double-edged destiny, either giving rise to interesting city sections, carefully outlining the themes of innovation in old places marked by historical memory, or producing flat monotonous landscapes, worn-out replicas of operations conceived and developed elsewhere, ones that depress instead of enlivening the zones to be reconverted.

In the places where the most convincing results have been obtained, action has been taken to ensure that several factors are in play – factors which are held to be essential components of the waterfront operation and which have also made significant contributions to the attainment of urban complexity, this being held to be the primary objective. Several criteria pertaining to these factors can be highlighted:

1 *The plurality of functions assigned to the area*, in relation to both its regeneration as well as its relationship with the rest of the city: in this sense the waterfront can play different but complementary roles. This means, for example, that it has been possible to assign to the waterfront the task of maintaining its character of border zone between water and city, while at the same time reinforcing the attributes of the central area which is closely linked to the heart of the city. Moreover, verification of the manner in which a process of more general urban redevelopment has sometimes been planned for is possible, placing the waterfront in the vanguard of change so that once consolidation has taken place on the seafront, certain conditions there can determine the development of the hinterland immediately behind the waterfront up to the more central zones, and, like a wave, spread development to more distant peripheral areas. The Barcelona experience, with the construction of the Olympic Village and the redefinition of the urban border along the seafront, continues, after almost ten years, to testify to the far-reaching scope of the project.

2 *The multiple activities in the redeveloped zones*. The mix of functions referring to the different sectors of the principal urban activities (economic-productive, residential, pertaining to culture and leisure, mobility), often represents the keystone of the success to redeveloping a waterfront. The difficulty, naturally, lies in the careful choice and the amount, so that the mix is not dominated by a single function or the consolidated dual term "commerce+entertainment," this being responsible for the degeneration of a certain model of waterfront organization which is particularly dear to many North American developers who entrust large commercial structures with the task of attracting visitors to these new areas which have finally been reappropriated for public use. Suitable antidotes for this danger of lowering the quality could be:

   • a significant number of *activities linked to previous and original uses* for these zones (for example, involving life at sea, fishing, navigation, and so on), with the purpose of keeping alive the memory of such unusual aspects, and preserving meaningful traces of the identity of these places;

- a careful arrangement of *productive activities*, compatible with the renewed context and capable of ensuring diversification in the zone's economy, with the capacity to guarantee diversification so that, for example, the traditional and the more innovative appear side by side. The latter may require only a little space and be easily accommodated in buildings previously used as factories or warehouses;
- the introduction of a quota for *residence and associated activities*, so that the waterfront and its immediate surrounds do not become a district dedicated exclusively to the flow of occasional visitors, thus creating another "specialized" area of the city that could affect the continuous, composite and heterogeneous fabric of the city by forming vast "picturesque" but artificial zones;
- an *outline of the routes* that facilitate and develop interaction between the different activities rather than separating them, so as to develop and encourage, especially along several pedestrian routes, a vast range of interchanges between the functions that contribute to accentuating the level of urban complexity.

3 *The co-presence of "public and private."* The more interesting water-front zones have an internal mix of these two "elements," mainly in reference to:

- the *functions*, so that alongside the activities usually referred to the public domain (e.g. headquarters of local government offices, museum structures, etc.) are those typically managed by the private sector (hotels, commercial structures, entertainment venues);
- the *spaces*, especially the open ones, with the purpose of joining traditional public spaces (plazas, roads, parks, cycle tracks and walking paths) and those controlled by the private sector (gardens, clubs, playing fields, etc.);
- the "*actors*" managing the services on the waterfront, as the different systems (and practices) of managing the zones and complexes situated in these areas help to recreate the typically urban mix of public and private activities.

The waterfront, a new laboratory of urban quality

When different cases of waterfront redevelopment are studied, it immediately becomes clear that one of the main objectives of these operations is to obtain a high qualitative level, both in terms of the physical-functional aspects as well as the environment as a whole. The results are sometimes worlds apart from the expectations and the outcomes quite different from images or descriptions in promotional material. Redeveloping the water-front becomes a challenge in the quest to enhance urban quality in the "construction" of the image of the modern city. In actual fact this quest is often directed at improving the layout and livability of the urban system as a whole: to attempt to limit the negative effects of vehicle traffic and introduce innovative means to satisfy the mobility needs of the city's residents, to re-acquire vast obsolete industrial zones, to revitalize run-down residential zones, and so on.

3.3 View of the London Docklands.

Waterfront redevelopment gives an insight into the way in which public administrations and private investors have acted (and continue to act) in reorganizing these abandoned areas. Focusing once again on the most significant projects in terms of results, several constant or sporadically used elements can be highlighted, with the aim of producing improved results for the operation as a whole:

1 *Opening up the waterfront to the public*, through a process that may entail successive phases of appropriation of the border zones between city and water (sea, river, lake). This is a prerequisite for all waterfront redevelopment operations, as very often appropriation by the city is seen as a necessary condition for commencing improvement work and attributing new value to these zones. Naturally public ownership of an area cannot in itself guarantee improved project quality, hence the guarantee of greater care and maintenance; in fact, it is often the opposite. Notwithstanding, in many waterfront redevelopment projects it is the actual opening to the public of a zone that was previously inaccessible that leads to a request for specific and high-level intervention.

2 *Development of accessibility to the waterfront*. Pedestrian access is essential, especially in relation to link routes with the city center and outlying zones. To achieve this, obstacles and impediments to circulation around the acquired area should be removed. High-level accessibility via public transport must also be guaranteed so that the waterfront is more easily reachable by various modes of land and water transport. It is essential that the main functions of pedestrian access be emphasized for the success of these operations, and all possible intersections of pedestrian routes with roads should be studied with great attention: the use of bridges, raised passageways or tunnels, renders access for pedestrians to the waterfront easier, safer and more pleasant.

3 *Limitations on vehicle traffic*: following redevelopment work, waterfronts have often become one of the city's main pedestrian zones, or, rather, the regeneration operation has often focused on making a good part of the waterfront a pedestrian area as one of its design objectives. One consequence is that the presence of private vehicle traffic has been

carefully studied so as to limit access, regulate the quantity and define routes accurately. Moving this type of traffic away entails a similarly clear choice for the development of public transport services (on road and rail, but also on water), so that the battle with the negative effects of the excessive use of private means in the city center (as happens in other prestigious urban zones such as the waterfront) is not transformed into a penalization for the mobility of residents and visitors, and thus becomes an option that is as radical as it is demagogic and fanciful.

4 *Upgrading waterborne transport* needs to be effected in two ways. The first, a "rediscovery" of this system of transport by the public, entails relaunching urban mobility through a full exploitation of the potential of waterborne means, and both relieves pressure on the city roads and makes transfers from one part of the city to another more pleasant, avoiding crossing the central zones. The second way is that of encouraging and improving modal interchanges between the different systems of land and water. The intermodal stations, between land and water, located naturally on the waterfront, can become complex urban structures, capable of hosting not only the functions linked to transport but other activities as well, making for an intense use of the services on offer, and able to attract flows of visitors and new users.

5 *Highlighted by the environmental and urban features of the waterfront*, to emphasize the unusual nature of this urban zone (its contact with the water, the views of the water and the city from this border zone, the presence of unusual consolidated activities, etc.), in order to make it appreciated by those who frequent it. Appropriate work on the embankments thus becomes of great relevance, as it does for the routes along the watersides, the piers, the wharves; special viewpoints must be chosen for enjoyment of the urban landscape and even modest elements salvaged to testify to the past. In this sense, the attention paid to the design of the furnishings for the waterfront can take on a special significance, which goes beyond the aesthetic aspect and aims to rediscover or introduce emblematic values referring to the presence of the water and its determining use in this zone.

6 *Ensuring the quality of the water* in the recovered waterfront zones. It is clear that this must cover all the bodies of water in the city; it is equally clear, however, that the redevelopment operation of the waterfront "land" zones is highly penalized, in both environmental and economic terms, if the body of water in front of the redeveloped areas is of unsatisfactory quality. High water quality, on the other hand, means the development of multiple uses, even though these are linked more to leisure time than to production; but the residential function, or the real estate activity in the wider sense, would be highly advantaged, as clean water can be seen as a sort of extension of the open area and usable by residents or visitors to the waterfront.

Waterfront: new urban "category" and globalization of the "phenomenon"

The aspects referred to in the preceding paragraphs are, as has been stated repeatedly, the result of careful observation. This observation leads

3.4 Parque do Flamengo in Rio de Janeiro.

to the conclusion that the waterfront has become a sort of new "category" in the picture of the elements that articulate and define the urban structure in the modern city which is characterized by a significant water presence. A typological "category" that can be placed alongside others which have been the subjects of considerable debate in the European countries in the past is the "central business district," a conceptual term to which the urban planning of the Old World was seriously committed several decades back. However, the continuing confrontation concerning the "historical centers" is also an important chapter in contemporary urban studies, which often theorize or practice development of the city "by parts," through sector policies, and often lose sight of the need for "concerted" and sympathetic growth among the different sectors – the need for development compatible between central and peripheral zones in order to create a profound unity of redevelopment for the whole of the urban organism.

The outstanding features of the waterfront redevelopment processes suggest that this type of area is of great "strategic" importance for the destiny of the city: a testing ground for verifying policies. In this sense, the waterfront can be seen as paradigmatic of the condition of the post-industrial city and its vicissitudes will make it possible for the fortunes and errors of urban policies to be interpreted.

Many cities have entrusted the waterfront with a serious task: to re-launch the city through the redevelopment of one area. This has taken place because the best-known and successful cases of waterfront projects have given rise to and directed a series of imitations, flat and ingenuous at times, which have multiplied and consolidated interest in this part of the city. Attentive administrations and alert entrepreneurs have attempted to define the features of the areas to be redesigned, emphasizing the most unusual characteristics, with the aim of constructing a new identity for the "place" which will be recognizable and will in turn act as a "model" in the field of waterfront redevelopment. Furthermore, it must be remembered that these projects also pose the problem of reconnecting relationships with the rest of the city and in particular with the center and the historic nucleus, correctly interpreting the need, mentioned earlier, for urban design plans and projects for reconnecting relationships or establishing new ones with other parts of the urban structure.

The formation of "models" of waterfront development, which took place on the basis of several successful cases which are now the focus of international literature, led to the spread of examples world-wide, and it is now appropriate to refer to a "globalization" of the waterfront themes. The "dangers," or rather the risks, of this are clear and are reminiscent of what happened in the field of shopping center construction, which experienced a revolution in the final period of the twentieth century; it ultimately led to uniformization on an international scale, not only of some construction standards but also of organizational methods, spatial typologies, and architectural forms, thus generating a monotonous sense of *déjà vu*, that makes places and structures impossible to distinguish. Because the waterfront is a part of the city and not a shopping center, suitable instruments for the analysis of the site to be redeveloped must be produced. This deserves to be emphasized, for although many waterfronts were areas of importance for ports in the past, they have not necessarily become urban zones in the meantime. In evaluating them, the traditional "tools of the trade" of the sector analysts (economists, urban planners, sociologists, etc.) should be avoided, at least in part, and an attempt made to "invent" and calibrate new methods for defining constraints on and the potential of waterfront projects.

It is important to remember that the theme of waterfront recovery isn't restricted to large cities. There are many medium and small urban centers which have areas adjacent to waterfronts, some being completely abandoned, others still involved in activities relating to fishing; the need for modernization and upgrading is pressing in these centers too. While the initial 25–30 years of work on waterfronts have mostly involved the large centers, there is no doubt that the great challenge will be played out over the coming decade in the thousands and thousands of towns and cities of more modest dimensions, all over the world, that will require greater attention and detailed study of their needs and development aims.

Waterfronts: models to be imitated or reference points to be studied?

In the way of thinking developing in many countries – namely, that of laying the foundations for the development of waterfronts in medium- and minor-sized towns – the issues of which path to take and which example to single out have become essential for the definition of a winning strategy for the projects to be effected. In this sense international literature, the countless conventions and the completed examples provide a broad and articulate picture of "approaches" and specific "solutions." Of these, following the initial US experiments in Baltimore and Boston, the complex and often innovative work at Vancouver and Sydney stand out. They have already received much in the way of comment, but deserve further study so that a full understanding of the outcomes is possible.

Three aspects of the Vancouver development are particularly worthy of evaluation: that of Granville Island and False Creek, Canada Place and the

Seabus line, linking the Downtown with the northern coast of Burrard Inlet in north Vancouver. Of great importance is the stress that a large city such as Vancouver has placed on the theme of waterborne transport, which is treated in textbook fashion in terms of its use and in the "creativity" of its development. On the other hand, Canada Place represents a consistent and daring example of a complex structure that can host activities closely related to both marine affairs and urban matters in a formal and exemplary synthesis. Granville Island has demonstrated an admirable capacity to restore life to a run-down zone, basing the design on an unusual combination of activities, mixed but distinct, resulting in a new and convincing arrangement for the island.

In Sydney as well, the long wave of waterfront redevelopment has led to interesting outcomes with plenty of novelties. The impact of the realization of Darling Harbour and the redevelopment process of the whole city was fundamental, not only for the dimension of the project itself, and the strategic position of the site, but essentially because the undertaking acted as a powerful renewal thrust for the entire zone west of the city. This process was concluded with the complex preparation for the 2000 Olympic Games at Homebush Bay.

Darling Harbour was the model for many other projects as it had a positive effect on the choice of combining different activities, even though there are differing opinions on the decision to create a district that mainly attracts occasional visitors in contrast to residents. However, there is no doubt that the Darling Harbour project has been a success. As a result, nearby redevelopment initiatives have been launched with the aim of bringing quality to the residential fabric of important zones such as the districts of Pyrmont and Ultimo.

In the meantime, on the international stage of waterfront redevelopment, other significant operations have taken place such as the Victoria & Alfred Waterfront in Cape Town, Puerto Madero in Buenos Aires, and the Barcelona seafront – these in addition to the celebrated projects in London's vast Docklands area, the Eastern Ports in Amsterdam, and Kop Van Zuid in Rotterdam. In reality, however, there are numerous interesting cases to be found in cities all over the world; some of the more inventive and experimental confirm that much can still be done in the field of waterfront redevelopment. One marvelous example comes from a city that is not usually thought of as having a waterfront, but which is closely linked to water due to the presence of two rivers and lakes inside the urban fabric: Berlin. A redevelopment experience has been under way for several years now, involving old industrial areas in direct contact with the water, thanks to a public company, Wasserstadt. With reference to results obtained elsewhere, but especially through the promotion of in-depth reflection on all the aspects concerning waterfront projects and alongside concrete action in the field, it is involving operators and experts from all over the world. In my opinion this is the most appropriate way to deal with the exciting challenge which is presented by land and water in cities over the coming years.

PART III
REMAKING THE IMAGE OF THE CITY

4 Remaking the image of the city
Bilbao and Shanghai

Richard Marshall

Competitive advantage has become the catch-cry of the modern era as more and more cities are forced to compete with each other for increasingly volatile capital. Competitive advantage is an essential aspect to many national, regional and local urban policy agendas. In a very direct way, this will impact the form of cities. Competition for market shares in the global economy will force major adjustments to the urban fabrics of cities as they rationalize to realize their economic potentials (Serageldin, 1997). Competition between cities is not new. Indeed cities have always competed for larger shares of capital and trade. What is new is the fact that in

4.1 Guggenheim Museum, Bilbao, on the edge of the river.

a world of unprecedented technological change and the development of a truly integrated global economy, the competition to attract wealth, in physical and human terms, is even more crucial. A city's success today depends less on location and more on the availability of an appropriate infrastructure (Marshall, 1998). A crucial aspect of these repositioning efforts is environmental and urban regeneration. Waterfront sites provide remarkable opportunities for redevelopment on large, highly centralized and therefore visible locations. It is this fact that makes waterfront development so important to many environmental and urban regeneration efforts.

The success of cities will not be achieved if the physical realm of the city is ignored. As cities shift from industrial to service economies, a major aspect of their success will be in the quality of their city spaces. Here the waterfront plays a critical role. In the first instance, waterfronts are often the most degraded places in the city, being the sites of the former industrial operations. Second, the waterfront is a highly visible location in most cities. Because of this waterfront development is crucial to the development of a city and also to the quality of its urban expression. The waterfront is that place in a city where designers and planners can forge contemporary visions of the city and in doing so articulate values that contribute toward urban culture.

Bilbao and Shanghai are two examples of how the waterfront has become the stage for a new expression of city aspirations. The new Bilbao and the new Shanghai are finding form along their respective waterfronts. Both cities have a long history of waterfront neglect, and yet today both cities are finding new forms of expression in these neglected zones. Bilbao is a case study in how a waterfront can provide opportunities for the creation of a new identity, a new expression of what the city is and wants to be. Shanghai, likewise, is a city in transition from an industrial character to one where issues of city quality are becoming critical.

In response to issues of competitive advantage, Shanghai has invested three times more in its urban infrastructure in the last five years than the total invested in the previous forty (Zhang Hui Min, 1999). These infrastructure projects include the construction of the Nanpu, Yangpu and Xupu bridges, Metro Line One, the elevated Inner Ring Road and North–South Elevated Road, as well as the Shanghai–Nanjing Expressway. Projects already approved or in planning include four new bridges, four new tunnels and a new walking bridge over and under the Huangpu.

In a matter of a decade, Shanghai has mushroomed as one of the world's biggest metropolises. This growth has come at an inevitable cost and the Shanghai Municipal Government has begun to address these negative conditions. As part of these considerations, two major redevelopments have been initiated along the Shanghai waterfront. The Suzhou Creek restoration is a major project to rehabilitate the industrial facilities that line the creek and to restore green areas along its banks. The Huangpu waterfront plan is an extensive redevelopment of port properties along the river. The waterfront in Shanghai is providing a once-in-a-lifetime opportunity to reposition the image of the city. It is providing Shanghai with an opportunity to present a new face to the world.

At the end of the 1980s, Bilbao faced many of the same issues as

Shanghai. Bilbao was an economic engine based on industrial output, which like many other cities around the world began to lose its economic vitality, and the city fell into decline. Sensing a bleak future, the Basque Country government decided to shift its economy from an industrial foundation to a service base in an effort to make the region, and the city of Bilbao, a central site within Europe's Atlantic façade. It initiated a revitalization plan, which included a series of strategic initiatives to improve investment in human resources, to create a service-oriented metropolis, and to engage in environmental and urban regeneration. Bilbao's is a remarkable story of renewal and its waterfront redevelopment efforts are at the core of its success.

The Bilbao context

The city of Bilbao, the capital of the Biscay province of the Basque Country on the Atlantic coast of northern Spain, is situated in the Euskadi, or Autonomous Community, of the Basque Country, on the northern edge of the Iberian Peninsula. It sits in the valley and estuary of the Nervión River, and this linear fold determines the stretched-out form of the city. Its population of nearly a million people spreads over thirty municipalities of unequal size. Six of these municipalities exceed 50,000 inhabitants: Bilbao, Barakaldo, Getxo, Portugalete, Santurtzi, and Basauri. Bilbao is the fifth most populated metropolitan area in Spain, behind Madrid, Barcelona, Valencia and Seville, and is comparable in size to cities such as Dublin, Liverpool or Florence.

The Villa of Bilbao was founded on June 15, 1300, when Don Diego López de Haro bestowed the Carta Magna to it. Little is known of the ancient history of the city; however, some historians speculate that it may have been the site of Roman Flaviogriga. During the twelfth and thirteenth centuries, before the foundation of the Villa, Bilbao was the main distribu-

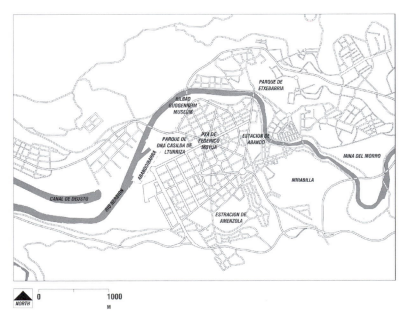

4.2 Map of Bilbao waterfront.

4.3 View of Bilbao.

tion point of Castillian products bound for the North Sea. This strategic commercial location led to the formation of the Villa. For some 300 years, the Town Hall and the Consulate, representing the University of Maritime Contractors and Merchants, dominated all commercial activity and civil society in the city. Bilbao acted as a nexus between the Europe of the North Atlantic and the interior kingdom of Castillia, as well as a connection between Seville and the Americas.

In the nineteenth century, Bilbao developed into an industrial center, with mining, iron and steel industries dominating the urban landscape. On the waterfront, shipping and railways carved their mark on the edge of the city. Because of its growing wealth, Bilbao grew both physically and politically. In the 1870s, the city annexed neighboring towns: first Abando, then Begoña, Deusto and Luchana. The city reached an economic peak, culminating in the 1920s, based on the sale of iron to England, some of which was destined for the manufacturing of arms for the First World War. The changes wrought by the Civil War in Spain and the growth of industry, brought thousands of immigrants from different parts of the country to Bilbao, creating both a ready workforce and also a very mixed cultural landscape.

In the 1960s and 1970s, with a crisis in manufacturing, the industrialized city fell into economic decline. Bilbao suffered from high unemployment, environmental decay, urban stagnation, and emigration. Under the rule of Franco, the city struggled politically to develop its competitive position. However, five years after his death, the Basque Country became a semi-autonomous region, free to set its own destiny and recast its relationship with the rest of Europe. The city's economic crisis and new bureaucratic autonomy coincided with the rise of cities and regions in a united Europe. Geopolitical lines between nation-states became blurry and the new economic circumstance of a united Europe began to favor autonomous regions.

In the early 1980s, the Basque Country government began to reposition its economy, moving away from its industrial foundation toward financial services and telecommunications. Bilbao Metropoli 30, a public–private institution, coordinated the revitalization. The plan included a series of strategic initiatives: to improve investment in human resources, to create a service-oriented metropolis, to improve mobility and accessibility, to engage in environmental and urban regeneration, to make Bilbao the center of culture in the region, to coordinate regeneration by involving both the public administration and the private sector, and, finally, to engage in social improvements for the people living in Bilbao.

Today, due to the success of its regeneration efforts, Bilbao is the banking capital of Spain and is aiming to be the informational technology portal for Europe. It is also home to the most impressive contemporary art museum of the decade – the Guggenheim Bilbao Museum. Recently, the European Union established a software institute in Bilbao to help its member nations compete with the United States and Japan. The city's hope is that it will become a magnet for high-tech business operations. Already, the Zamodio Technological Park, located northeast of the city, houses thirty-eight start-up companies in biotechnology, telecommunications, software, and robotics.

The Shanghai context

The city of Shanghai, located along the Huangpu River, is the largest city in China and one of the largest in the world with a population of some 14 million people. The metropolis is composed of ten rural districts and twelve city districts. Since the opening of China and the transition to a socialist market economy, Shanghai has mushroomed. The city is now the largest construction site on the planet. There are currently 4,000 buildings over twenty-four stories in the city with another 1,700 either under construction or in planning approval (Zhao Wan Liang, 2000). The city is divided into East Shanghai, Pudong, and West Shanghai, Puxi. Puxi is the old part of the city, a great arc on the west side of the Huangpu River fronted by

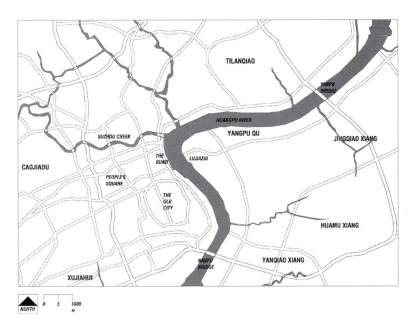

4.4 Map of Shanghai waterfront.

4.5 View across the Huangpu River, Shanghai, looking toward Puxi.

the famous Bund. The Pudong is the new Shanghai, with the Oriental Pearl TV Tower sitting in front of new high-rise office towers. The heart of the old city is located a few blocks west of the Bund around Nanjing Road and Yunan East Road. The cultural center of the city is located around Renmin (People's) Square, The Temple of the City God and Yu Yuan Garden. Situated in the Jiangsu province, the city sits on the alluvial plain of the Yangtze River; the name "Shanghai" literally translates as "upriver to the sea."

Shanghai began as a fishing village some 700 years ago during the Tang and Song Dynasties. Even 150 years ago it was subordinate in size and influence to other cities such as Suzhou and Hanzhou. Its rise to dominance is related to its role as a treaty port. Its location, at the confluence of the Yangtze and Huangpu Rivers, led to it becoming a commercial shipping port, and as international trade increased during the Ming Dynasty (1368–1644), Shanghai became a major town in southeast China. For hundreds of years, the Emperors of China actively isolated the Middle Kingdom from the rest of the world. Although China had some international trade contacts, they decreed that China was totally self-sufficient and simply did not need nor want outside contact. The end of China's isolation came at the end of the Opium Wars with the Treaty of Nanking in 1842.

After the First Opium War, China ceded Hong Kong to the British and five other cities were opened up to Western trade, namely Guangzhou, Xiamen, Fuzhou, Ningpo and Shanghai. By the turn of the century, there were around fifty such foreign enclaves, the most important being Shanghai. The British chose Shanghai as a strategically located safe harbor. Under the Treaty of Nanking, Shanghai became an international business center and the British were soon joined by other foreigners, namely the French (1847), Americans (1863) and the Japanese (1895). In the "International Settlement," foreigners were allowed to establish their own laws and use their own security forces. By 1853, Shanghai was the busiest Chinese port and had a population of some 50,000. By the turn of the century, its population had grown to one million people.

The establishment of Shanghai as a treaty port led to the creation of foreign concessions. The West Bank of the Huangpu, known to foreigners as the Bund and to the locals as Waitan, soon became a new-development area. Under the "Land Regulations" issued by the Shanghai Magistrate the British settlement extended from Suzhou Creek at the north to the Yang King Pang Creek in the south. The French concession extended from Yang King Pang Creek to the city walls. According to the "Land Regulations," the foreign land lease agreements were required to leave a space of thirty English feet between the buildings and the edge of the river as a towpath, for pulling boats out of the water, and a sidewalk. This stretch of mud, as it was in those days, soon became one of the most striking civic districts in the world, filled with Georgian, Victorian, Gothic and Queen Anne architecture, which survives as a remarkable legacy today.

Until the 1930s, Shanghai enjoyed the coexistence and incorporation of different cultures with the different regional Chinese cultures. The introduction of foreign capital and the rise of national industry and commerce accelerated the development of the city and its economy, making Shanghai a major economic and cultural metropolis in the early part of the twentieth century. After the civil war and the People's Revolution of 1949, Chinese control was reimposed over all of Shanghai. As Rimmington notes, the new regime, while prepared to make use of the city's industrial and commercial know-how as a model of development across the country, rejected all the remnants of colonialism and consumerism. This, combined with a focus on rural development, meant that much of the pre-revolution development in the city came to an end (Rimmington, 1998:25).

Under Chinese control, Shanghai became an industrial powerhouse and the economic engine for all of China. In Mao's time, from 1950 to 1976, Shanghai sent thirteen times more revenue to the central government than the amount it received for the city budget. In fact, as late as 1984 Shanghai still gave more than 85 percent of its budgetary revenue to Beijing (White and Cheng, 1998:36). Figures from 1982 suggest that Shanghai produced eleven times the level of gross domestic product per capita than all of China combined (Meier, 1982).

Shanghai faced three major challenges in the period of open reform in the 1990s. The revenue sent to Beijing had left Shanghai with little money to update urban infrastructure. Shanghai was in desperate need of new road construction, better transportation, improved water supply, housing and an improvement in the environmental quality of the city and rivers. In addition, Shanghai was desperate for new investment, especially in the Pudong area. Because of these problems, Shanghai's position as the economic engine for China suffered and the city's competitive advantage slipped.

4.6 View down the Huangpu River, Shanghai, from the Pearl Television Tower.

In response to this, the city started an aggressive remaking of itself. Capital was created through the "transfer of land rights," which became the prime source of raising money in the late 1980s. Land rents replaced extractions from state firms as the primary means of municipal capital generation for urban construction. Revenue generated in this way was equivalent to sixty percent of Shanghai's total fixed investment for 1993 (White and Li, 1998). In addition, in the late 1980s Shanghai borrowed US$1.4 billion, with approval from Beijing, for urban construction projects such as the Shanghai Metro and the new Huangpu Bridge.

Remaking the image of the city

The appearance of Bilbao, characterized by a harsh relationship between its built fabric and its topography, is one of extremely dense urban areas, industrial complexes, a mixture of domestic architecture and layers of transportation facilities standing in stark contrast to the rolling green landscape. The remaking of the city involves the removal of the former industrial facilities strewn along the riverfront. This will change the nature of the role of the river in the city. The backbone of the city will be the Nervión River, a waterway that is already starting to lose its harsh and polluted character. The port of Bilbao was originally located in the center of the city, but recently activity has been shifted to the outer port. The old sulfurous shipyards will disappear and most of the port and industrial activities will relocate to the El Abra Bay, transforming the Nervión Ría into a linear core for the new metropolitan territory. This stitching of the city will bring together the communities along the riverbank, from Casco Viejo to Algorta on the right bank, passing through Deusto, Las Arenas and Neguri, to the left bank from Ensanche to Santruce, passing through Baracaldo, Sestao and Portugalete.

The Nervión Ría will no longer be a physical and social boundary in the city. The recently completed subway system, whose tunnels run next to the watercourse, will tie the river along its length and introduce seven new bridges. The recovery of the riverbanks, by the removal of obsolete struc-

4.7 The edge of the river in Bilbao.

tures and railways, opens a new system of urban spaces and linear parks along the river. Historically the city has always treated the river as a back. The new condition of the river, however, transforms the Nervión Ría into a major feature for the city and in doing so repositions the image of the city.

The remaking of the image of the city is being propelled by a series of important projects. These include the development of transport infrastructures, the cleaning of the river, and urban development along the waterfront. The centerpiece of the city's Master Plan is the redevelopment of the Abandoibarra, a 70-acre site in the former industrial port and rail station extending along the Nervión River within a five-minute walk from downtown. This new cultural district is formed by the Museo de Bella Artes, the University de Duesto and the Old Town Hall. The site is bisected by the Puente de la Salve, a vehicular entry into Bilbao. A public–private initiative, called Bilbao Ría 2000, the scheme includes an office tower to house the County Government of Biscay, residential and retail facilities, a new Sheraton hotel, a university library, a new Congress Hall, a sea and river museum, and the new Bilbao Guggenheim Museum.

Located on the eastern edge of the Abandoibarra site, facing the river, the Bilbao Guggenheim Museum has placed the city in the mainstream of the international art world. The architects invited to participate in the international design competition were Frank O. Ghery, Coop Himelbau and Arata Isozaki. Frank O. Ghery was awarded the commission and the notoriety of the completed building, opened in October of 1997, has focused international interest on Bilbao and served to reposition the city as a world-class metropolis. The museum comprises a series of interconnected

4.8 The Guggenheim Museum, Bilbao.

shapes which are clad in limestone and unified by a curving, twisting tita-nium roof. The building establishes an unprecedented presence against the background of the Puenta de la Salve, the Nervión River, the surround-ing hills, and the grayness of the downtown. This building has been hailed as a masterpiece of contemporary architecture, and indeed the project has come to represent the renaissance of the entire city. The project is responsible for bringing US$210 million of increased economic revenue to the region, of which US$30 million has gone to the Government of Biscay in taxes.

Other major projects in the regeneration of the city include the Confer-ence and Concert Hall, designed by Federico Soriano and Dolores Palacios, located just west of the Abandoibarra area, next to the Euskalduna Bridge; Sir Norman Foster and Associates designed the underground stations for the Metro Bilbao; a new airport designed by Santiago Calatrava; and Michael Wilford designed the Abando Passenger Interchange. Although the interchange project is currently on hold it comprises a complex of resi-dential and service facilities combined with local, inter-city and high-speed trains, bus and underground connections and car parking. The Bilbao Harbor Extension is a major infrastructure improvement to the port, making Bilbao Spain's leading merchant shipping port with Europe's deepest docking facilities (105 feet).

The ultimate aim is to create a logistical Activities Zone that will serve as a nucleus for the Zamudio Technology Park and the European Software Institute. These projects are evidence of Bilbao's commitment to high-tech industries. Also important in these regeneration projects is the clean-up of the Nervión River, which will improve the quality of water and bring life back to the river by 2004. To date, one-third of the 12-mile waterfront has been renewed to the European Union "Blue Flag" level, another third has been cleaned to 50 percent and the final third has been cleaned to 25 percent. Other cities now look to the success of the Bilbao revitalization and the city is active in networking with other European cities immersed in

4.9 The Calatrava Bridge, Bilbao.

revitalization projects, such as the Eurocities project, and internationally with cities such as Pittsburgh.

The Strategic Plan for the Revitalization of Metropolitan Bilbao was initiated in 1989 at the request of the Basque Government and the Biscay County Council. The intention of this plan was to shape Metropolitan Bilbao for the next century. Some critical aspects of the plan include:

- Investment in human resources with a focus on educational and training programs in order to generate competitive advantages for business development in the city.
- The need to diversify the economic base to establish Bilbao as a service metropolis in a modern industrial region, which included the development of the Stock Exchange, the development of the Port for advanced maritime activities, the availability of an international Exhibition Center and the development of the European Software Institute. Such initiatives represent key nodes in the competitive position of the metropolis.
- The communications system for the Metropolitan Area, which incorporates a system of internal mobility that would allow adequate connection among different sub-regions. The development of the public transport system, mentioned earlier, new highways and rail connections leading to the rest of Europe were initiated under the direction of the Plan. The new Port at the Exterior Abra and the development of the Airport in Sondika extend the possibilities of regional, national and international connections for the city.
- The image of Metropolitan Bilbao's environment as a central concern. The Revitalization Plan promoted the control and management of air and water quality and the efficient management of waste products (urban and industrial), according to European Union standards. Regeneration of environmentally degraded areas was a crucial factor for the improvement of the city's external image and hence competitive position.
- Fostering a social and cultural centrality. This includes various emblematic buildings which contribute to improving the external image of the city, the best known of which is the Guggenheim Museum. The revitalization of the image of the city includes, as well, the redevelopment of decaying urban infrastructure and the rehabilitation of the old town.

Urban regeneration is a success in Bilbao due to an internal awareness of the need for improvement and the generation of a new external image to attract development. The recovery of the estuary as an axis of the metropolis and its sanitation has already led to a decisive improvement in the quality of life and attractiveness of the city. It has become the supporting artery for the new central areas of the city. Given the central position of the Estuary within the design of new Metropolitan Bilbao, it was therefore essential to promote the regeneration of the Abandoibarra area, mentioned previously.

• Culture is fundamental to the revitalization of the city. The intention is to make Bilbao a "Center of Art and Congresses." In this way, elements that contribute to the generation of this image are considered in the same way as urban infrastructure. The University, Guggenheim Museum of Bilbao, Euskalduna Concert and Conference Hall, and the Cultural Center are the infrastructural elements that define the cultural position of the city.

The Bilbao experience of urban regeneration is simply remarkable. A key element in Bilbao's success is the understanding that the potential of the city can only be fully realized through a coordinated effort between the public administration and the private sector. This has led to the development of "territorial planning" for the metropolitan area and the reinforcement of municipal urban management practices. The aim of the Revitalization Plan was always the creation of "common wealth" for all the citizens of Metropolitan Bilbao. The idea of "social action" and of personal well-being is a fundamental priority of urban development in the city (Asociacion Para La Revitalizacion Del Bilbao Metropolitano, 1999). A new plan developed in 2000 emphasizes the "softer" aspects of the infrastructure more than the provision of physical infrastructure.

The redevelopment of the Shanghai waterfront

Shanghai is similar to Bilbao in that it suffered an economic decline due to a downturn in its industrial production. As part of a city-wide redevelopment program its waterfronts are the focus for one of the most extensive public realm improvements in the world. Shanghai has an urban form, which is typical of cities in the south of the lower reaches of the Yangtze River. It might be described as a circular form with a chessboard road system. Its history as a Treaty Port has left a legacy of residual European urban patterns within the fabric of the city. Shanghai's waterfronts are an important aspect of the city's morphology. There are 697 square kilometers of water area and more than 3,000 rivers, creeks and streams in the metropolitan area of Shanghai. The city's industrial activities have heavily polluted many of these waterways. However, as part of the general urban improvement of the city there has been a concerted effort to improve the quality of these water systems.

Since 1990, Shanghai has undergone unprecedented, rapid and large-scale development. The transition from planned economy to socialist market economy, from the free use of land to the paid use of land, has required an appropriate adjustment of the city's layout and function. In

4.10 The mouth of Suzhou Creek, Shanghai, from the Pearl Television Tower.

line with this, the Shanghai Municipal People's Government obtained the approval of Beijing to open and develop the Pudong area in the early 1990s. In January of 1993, the Shanghai Pudong New Area Administration was established. The Pudong covers some 200 square miles of land and includes some 2.5 million people.

4.11 View of the Shanghai model.

4.12 View across the Bund, Shanghai.

The area of the Pudong includes the Finance and Trade Zone (known as Lu Jia Zui), the Free Trade Zone (called Waigaoqiao), the Export Processing Zone, Jingqiao, a High Technology Park, Zhangjiang, a new Port, the new Shanghai Hongqiao International Airport, an Info Port and the Pudong Railway.

The city center in Puxi is also a major focus of renewal efforts. The Municipal Government established five main considerations for the rede-velopment of Shanghai, based upon transportation infrastructure, a multi-centered city layout, the renovation of industrial areas, urban housing, and ecological projects. The first transportation infrastructure projects included the construction of the Nan Pu, the Yang Pu, and the Shi Pu Bridges, the Cross Harbor Tunnel, the Inner Ring Road, and the North–South Elevated Road. There are plans to construct a total of 400 miles of expressway around Shanghai. In addition, as part of a comprehensive transportation policy, six miles of new transit line are to be constructed every year.

Urban housing was a major issue in the redevelopment plans and to date 1.5 million people have been accommodated over a period of ten years. These developments include the construction of new housing and the renovation of older areas in the city. Ecological concerns are increasing in importance in Shanghai and the government has initiated several meas-ures to address air pollution, solid waste production, the treatment of wastewater and the greening of urban areas.

The Shanghai waterfront consists of the Huangpu River and the Suzhou Creek. In the period of massive industrial production, Shanghai's water-ways were lined with industrial facilities, port operations and warehouses. Because of the lack of pollution containment the water quality of those waterways was very poor. Several measures are changing the nature of waterfronts in Shanghai. The most significant is the relocation of major port functions from the Huangpu to the Yangtze River, allowing for major sections of the Huangpu to be redeveloped.

In 1993, the waterfront on the Bund was reconstructed. This involved the construction of a high embankment wall to protect against flooding which incorporated a pedestrian riverbank three-quarters of a mile long adjacent to the famous roadway. Since the early 1990s, the Bund has lost many of its trees and, with the rapid development of the city, the boulevard has become a congested traffic artery.

The main stream of Shanghai, named by foreigners as Suzhou Creek and historically called the Woosung River, flows down into the Huangpu River from Tai Lake, the third largest lake in China. Within Shanghai itself, the Creek runs through the very heart of the city. The Creek serves as flood release, water drainage, navigation channel, and provides irrigation as well as being a fishery. The banks of the Creek historically consisted of factories and warehouses. Not surprisingly, it has therefore suffered from a significant pollution problem. Untreated effluent from the factories turned the water of Suzhou Creek black. At the confluence of the two rivers, the black water contrasted markedly with the waters of the Huangpu. With recent efforts to improve the water quality of the Creek this phenomenon has been reduced.

Suzhou Creek divides Puxi into two parts. The northern part was the former Chinese territory, and a small part in the east end was the American Settlement, established in 1848. The southern part was the former British Settlement, established in 1846. Suzhou Creek became the contact point between the Chinese City and the International Settlements. This condition explains some of the traffic problems now present in this part of the city. Movement east and west is relatively easy; however, movement north and south (that is, across the Creek) is difficult (Shiling, 1998). The reason for this is that the Creek was historically the back-side for both the Chinese City and the British Concession. This fact also explains the random nature of the street organization in the area and the reason that the districts around the Creek were crowded and disorganized. Indeed, the character of the Creek was always one of pollution, noise and crime.

In 1997, as part of a wider remaking of the image of the city, a renewal project for Suzhou Creek started. As part of this, a one and a half mile green belt was constructed and a grand project is now underway to create a park around the Creek. The project includes the preservation of historic buildings, the reorganization of the traffic system, the creation of parks, the establishment of water platforms and the reconstruction of the riverbank. With the improvement of the water quality in the Creek, the famously black and odorous waters will become an aspect of the past.

The regeneration of the Huangpu River is the larger waterfront development and will significantly change the nature of the city. The Shanghai P&K Development Company joined the Shanghai Port Authority to create the development framework for investment, marketing and coordination of the Huangpu waterfront. In collaboration with the Shanghai Urban Planning and Urban Research Institute, Skidmore Owings and Merrill International Ltd. prepared the redevelopment scheme. With the opening of the Pudong, the Huangpu shifted from being the eastern edge of the city to becoming the center of the city. It now exists as the join between Puxi and Pudong, the old and new Shanghai. The scheme focuses on the redevelopment of port properties now that major port functions have shifted to the Yangtze River. Currently only a small section of the waterfront on the Huangpu is accessible and the primary motive of the plan was to extend this accessibility to make the waterfront an asset for all. The

4.13 Design Master Plan, Shanghai.

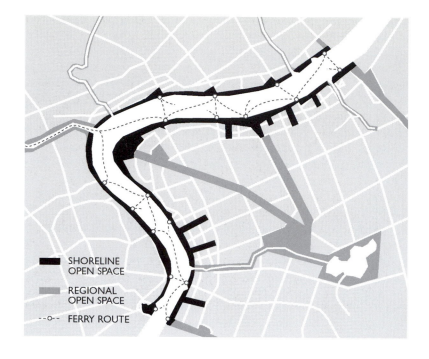

SHORELINE
OPEN SPACE

REGIONAL
OPEN SPACE

--○-- FERRY ROUTE

4.14 Artist's impression of the new Shanghai waterfront (1).

redevelopment aims to make the waterfront the heart of the city's cultural, social and civic life. The waterfront has, for a very long time, been looked at as a nasty, polluted environment by the residents of Shanghai. With the relocation of many industries and stricter environmental controls the water quality has improved to a point where people once again desire to be at the water's edge.

The plan aims at extending the visual and physical linkages from the water to the city. This is achieved by extending streets and neighborhood parks to link the waterfront to a larger system of regional parks and open spaces. In addition, access and connections in the city are extended by the location of transit terminals adjacent to the waterfront and the incorporation of extensive pedestrian networks. Movement on the water creates another level of vitality on the river. River ferry, coastal ferry and ocean ferry terminals are incorporated into the plan. The success of the scheme lies in the creation of a series of distinct neighborhoods with specific characteristics to lend them identity. These include the Crescent, a large cultural gathering space, Pier 16, a coastal passenger terminal, and a Resort Area.

4.15 Artist's impression of the new Shanghai waterfront (2).

Conclusion

Too often in architecture we focus on the end-product and ignore the process that laid the foundation for its creation. This is certainly the case in Bilbao. The power and beauty of Gerhy's Guggenheim veils the planning efforts of a multitude of individuals extending over more than a decade. Bilbao's success is remarkable, not only because of its great architecture but also for the communal vision and strength of conviction it displayed almost twenty years ago. Who would have thought that the museum of the decade, if not the century, would be in the industrial center of the Biscay province! Bilbao's story is a remarkable one for how a city with a

4.16 The Nervión River, Bilbao.

gritty, industrial character can rework that image to become the banking center for Spain and a major center of culture in all of Europe.

The image of Bilbao was a central concern of the revitalization efforts. The revitalization plan promoted the redevelopment of the environmentally degraded areas and the urban structure for both the competitive advantage Bilbao was seeking for itself, and also for the quality it aspired to be as a place. The Bilbao waterfront was the stage upon which these efforts became physical. The revitalization of the image of the city included, as well, the redevelopment of damaged urban infrastructure and the rehabilitation of the old town. The success of urban regeneration in the Metropolitan Area of Bilbao developed from an awareness of the need for an atmosphere of cooperation between all parties in the city. The generation of a new external image is essential in order to attract development, and the remaking of the waterfront is a critical aspect of this generation. The redevelopment of the estuary as an axis within the metropolis has led to an improvement in the quality of life and attractiveness of the city.

The Bilbao revitalization efforts are also remarkable for their comprehensiveness. In the American context, such communal cooperation is rare, and

4.17 Puente de la Salve, Bilbao.

4.18 View toward Puxi and the Bund, Shanghai.

too often political and jurisdictional fragmentation thwarts the development of good urban policy. In Bilbao, over a period of some fifteen years, the clarity of the vision and the commitment to its execution was unwavering. Despite political and administrative changes the progress of the revitalization plan was never impaired. The success of such commitment and cooperation is now evident.

Shanghai shares many of the same elements as Bilbao. The city is, of course, an international business, trade and finance center. Its role as gateway to China has secured it a competitive position within the hierarchy of cities in the Pacific Rim. Shanghai, however, recognized the need for a vast improvement in its urban infrastructure. This occurred at about the same time as in Bilbao and its development program is simply phenomenal. For those of us in the American context, the extent of infrastructure under construction in Shanghai is staggering. Likewise, the speed of this construction is hard to imagine. We are inclined, perhaps naturally, to view such construction with cynical eyes. Indeed, North American central cities have after all been in decline for some time now, even when our suburban sprawl is expanding at astonishing rates. The development of Shanghai is analogous to the tremendous expansions that occurred in North America over a hundred years ago. Indeed the dynamics of development are similar in terms of the desire to provide infrastructure to a large population in a very short amount of time.

As planners and architects, the thought of building a city suitable for the habitation of 14 million people is completely paralyzing; yet the city administration of Shanghai simply has no choice. Given the speed and size of the construction in Shanghai it is somewhat comforting to realize that issues of environmental regeneration and urban redevelopment are playing so heavily on the minds of decision-makers. There is a commitment to

4.19 View toward Pudong and Lu Jia Zui, Shanghai.

issues of quality, particularly in terms of the waterfront, that suggests hope for a better urban environment in Shanghai. One indeed hopes that this commitment is a long-term one. One also hopes that, as was the case in Bilbao, Shanghai is able to develop an inspired vision for itself.

"Remaking the Image of the City" was based in part upon case material prepared by researchers at the Harvard Graduate School of Design and presentations by Zhang Hui Min, Director of Shanghai Municipal Construction Commission; the President of the Provincial Council of Biscay, Josu Bergara Etxebarria; Juan Ignacio Vidarte, the Director of the Guggenheim Bilbao Museum; and Luis Rodriguez Llopis, Director of the Bilbao Office of IDOM at the Waterfronts in Post Industrial Cities Conference, 7–9 October, 1999, Harvard Design School, Cambridge, Massachusetts.

References

Association for the Revitalization of Metropolitan Bilbao (1999) http://www.brn30.es/

http://www.bilbao.net

Bartolucci, Marisa (1996) "Bilbao," in *Metropolis* (New York), 16 (1) July–Aug.: 63, 99.

Editorial Note, in Werk, Bauen + Wohnen, 1996, Dec., n. 12, pp. 2–5.

Giovannini, Joseph (1997) "Reshaping Bilbao," *Architecture DC*, 86 (12), Dec.: 39–40.

Larrauri, Eva (1999) "Bilbao Renace de las Cenizas de su Industria," *El Pais*, June 1 (Barcelona edition).

Marshall, R. (1998) Kuala Lumpur: Competition and the Quest for World City Status, *Built Environment*, 24 (2): 271–279.

Meier, R. (1982) *Shanghai: An Introduction to its Future*, Institute of Urban and Regional Development, UC Berkeley Working Paper No. 395, November.

Rimmington, D. (1998) "History and Culture," in Hook, B. (ed.) *Shanghai and the Yangtze Delta: A city reborn*, Oxford, New York: Oxford University Press, 1–29.

Serageldin, I. (1997) A decent life. *Harvard Design Magazine*, Winter/Spring, p. 25.

Shiling, Z. (1998) *Shanghai, An Everchanging Metropolis*, Shanghai: Tongji University.

White, L. and Cheng, L. (1998) "Government and Politics," in Hook, B. (ed.) *Shanghai and the Yangtze Delta: A city reborn*, Oxford, New York: Oxford University Press, 30–73.

Zhang Hui Min (1999) Presentation at Waterfronts in Post Industrial Cities, at Harvard Design School, 8 October.

Zhao Wan Liang (2000) Discussion between Zhao Wan Liang, Senior Urban Planner and Richard Marshall, at the Shanghai Urban Planning and Design Research Institute, Shanghai, 28 June.

Instant China – Notes on an urban transformation, 2G no. 10, Editorial Gustavo Gili, SA, 1999.

Atlas of Shanghai (1997) Shanghai Scientific and Technical Publishers.

5 Waterfronts as catalysts for city renewal

Martin L. Millspaugh

At the turn of the Millennium, the renewal of urban waterfronts can be seen as a keynote of economic development in post-industrial cities around the world, and the model for that phenomenon which is mentioned most often may be the Baltimore Inner Harbor Redevelopment in an old industrial port city in the northeastern "rust-belt" megalopolis of the US. A city which has lost almost 30 percent of its 1945 population and suffered from all of the urban lifestyle crises of the twentieth century,

5.1 Before the harbor redevelopment, Baltimore.

Baltimore has nevertheless rekindled its spirit and created a distinctive international image for itself through a systematic, entrepreneurial and beautiful makeover of its old Inner Harbor – where the still-important Port of Baltimore had its beginnings in the early 1700s.

During the Second World War, Baltimore's shipyards and steel mills made the city a key component in America's Arsenal of Democracy, but after the war it receded into anonymity as a self-contained industrial satellite of Washington, DC. The people withdrew into an ingrown cocoon with a small-town character that was nurtured by the pleasant life on the shores of Chesapeake Bay, but suffered from a collective inferiority complex when exposed to the outside world. This state of withdrawal was rudely shattered in 1953, when a respected private economic watchdog commission reported that the flight to the suburbs was causing property values in the central city to shrink at the rate of 10 percent a year, and municipal bankruptcy was foreseen within ten years if something was not done to reverse the trend.

Something was done, in the form of the Charles Center–Inner Harbor Redevelopment Program, created by one of the first generic public–private partnerships of the post-industrial age in the US. The results were eye-opening. Between 1960 and 1995 more than a hundred large and small development projects were completed, ranging from museum-quality sculpture to 35-story corporate headquarters buildings.

In all, over 12 million square feet of floor area has been constructed (more than three times what was considered achievable when the Master Plan was announced), upwards of $3 billion has been invested in public, private and non-profit construction, and property values in the key blocks at the Inner Harbor's focal point have increased by as much as 600 percent. More than 15,000 jobs were created or attracted by the revitalization program, and Moody's bond service had increased the city's rating from A to A-1 by the halfway mark in 1977.

Even more dramatically, a critical mass of attractions clustered around the Inner Harbor created a new tourism industry where none had existed before. Fourteen million annual local visits are now swelled by 6.5 million tourists who spent almost $3 billion in the city in 1999. When the Hyatt Regency Hotel opened in the early 1980s – the first of twelve hotels bringing 3,500 new rooms to the Inner Harbor – it quickly became the most successful property in the Hyatt chain.

The transformation was hard-earned. More than 1,000 properties had to be acquired for redevelopment, and 730 businesses were relocated – more than 90 percent of them in the city limits. But in the end, 75 percent of the new investment came from the private sector, and the quasi-public management process, or "delivery system," cost the taxpayers less than 3 percent of the public capital invested in the program.

The world has taken notice. The Inner Harbor redevelopment program has received more than forty national or international awards for planning, design and implementation. Baltimore was named one of the top ten growth markets in the US by *Advertising Age* magazine, selected as an All-American City by the National Municipal League, and singled out as the city with the best urban revitalization program by the International Federation for Housing and Planning. An institute award from the

American Institute of Architects said it all in 1984 when it described the Inner Harbor as "one of the supreme achievements of large-scale urban design and development in U.S. history." In 1991, the international Waterfront Center simply listed the Inner Harbor as "one of the top 10 waterfront places in the world." As luck would have it, the 35-year period of development was observed and documented by a few individuals who remain on the scene, and one of them has compiled the reflections and description of lessons learned that follows below.

Abandonment of the old ports

It seems fortuitous, but nevertheless positive, that the Millennium has arrived at a time when the cities of the world are enjoying a surge of benefits – such as those experienced in Baltimore – from the maturing of the waterfront development movement. The huge success of cities such as Baltimore is persuading other cities to undertake or accelerate their planning and infrastructure construction to create waterfront activity and profitable, tax-producing urban centers. This is equally true of famous international cities and of urban centers in underdeveloped countries.

In many if not most cities, central city revitalization means waterfront development: after all, what important city is not located on a waterfront of some sort – and for very good reasons! The basis for this movement began in the years after the Second World War, when the emergence of the container shipping industry accelerated the abandonment of old ports all over the world. The old ports were too crowded, and their piers had too little dockside land area for the flow of containers; as a result, in port city after port city, deep-sea shipping has moved out of the city center, abandoning the historic old port area where the city began, and where the city's image was created for the rest of the world.

This clearly opened up a great opportunity for new development, but with some problems or hurdles to overcome. First, of course, all ports are geographically subject to natural forces – tides, hurricanes, siltation, pollution – in a way that other urban development sites are not. Second, the abandoned piers and warehouses were surrounded by industrial properties which were also abandoned by maritime-related businesses, and the waterfront provided space where the construction of railroads and superhighways found the path of least resistance, cutting off the center of the city permanently from the water. As a result, whole port areas are shunned by public and private users and developers of other types of real estate.

In the last few years, the abandonment of old port areas has been reinforced by the growing concern for environmental problems: the old ports contain many forms of contamination of water, land and air, and the cost of eliminating those conditions often makes waterfront development too expensive to be economically feasible. Finally, there are liable to be intergovernmental rivalries that can create major problems for development in a situation where fifteen or twenty different authorities must give their consent for any new construction. Port authorities and municipal governments seem to have a natural tendency to disagree on goals and objectives for new development – or at least on the territorial question of who has the right to be in charge.

5.2 First version of Baltimore's Inner Harbor Plan.

For all of these reasons, the old streets and utilities along the waterfront are likely to be obsolete or inadequate, and the bulkhead or sea wall along the water's edge probably needs to be rebuilt. Because of the overall image of abandonment and obsolescence, an old port is liable to be perceived as a community's back door, which tends to discourage any new users or investors from tackling the difficult and costly job of development or redevelopment of port properties. This in turn discourages the public sector from investing the large capital sums for infrastructure work that must precede any significant private construction.

A priceless opportunity

Still, in spite of all the obstacles, urban waterfronts have the potential to create unmatched opportunities for redevelopment – the creation of new uses in place of the blighted, abandoned property that once held the city's industrial heart.

In the first place, geographically, most of the old ports can benefit from a central location. Since the old port is usually where a city started, it is found in or near the geographic center of the region, and this brings the advantage of easy access for the public transportation system – whether it be highways, local streets, or public mass transit. The center of the region is likely to be familiar to the majority of residents of the area; in fact, it may be clearly visible across a body of water unencumbered by other buildings. Second, the abandonment of the inner port areas has created a huge reservoir of unoccupied dockside property. As less expensive methods for curing the inevitable contamination are discovered (or legislated), the result will be to increase greatly the number of those waterfront sites that can be made available for development. Third, since the piers and head-houses were part of the original city, they are likely to be surrounded by the city's oldest and most beautiful neighborhood of buildings, streets and plazas – surroundings which provide an ideal setting for redevelopment of the abandoned property with new uses, especially those that are generated by the growing need of the people of the world for new and expanded leisure and recreational facilities. Finally, there is simply the presence of water: it has a magical quality that attracts and moves the human spirit like no other element. The presence of a sizeable body of water gives all port areas an emotional appeal which is ideal for recreation, entertainment and cultural activities – which in economic terms create the foundations for tourism as well as for leisure activities of the local population.

So while the abandonment of an old port by deep-sea shipping may seem a short-term negative in terms of attracting capital to a city, it actually opens up a priceless opportunity to create a new image, or marquee, for a city or a region – a new waterfront focal point that will be a signal for people to once again enjoy the visceral pleasure of coming to the

5.3 Baltimore: 1975 Plan.

water's edge, and to share that pleasure with visitors or tourists. Today, this opportunity is enhanced in many ways by emerging trends in the areas of technology, public policy and human behavior that favor the growth of waterfront development.

Emerging trends

The first of these trends comes about because of the changing technology of office work, expressed in an evolution of the functions of the Central Business District (CBD). The need for ever more offices, which used to fill those downtown skyscrapers quickly, is shrinking while the demand for new office space is moving outward, to be dispersed over the entire metropolitan region. The causes are obvious: they include the computerization of the daily office routine, the ever-increasing reliance on the private automobile for commuting, and the high cost of storing private vehicles on expensive downtown land. In place of the reduced demand for offices and the service industries that go along with them, city planners and developers

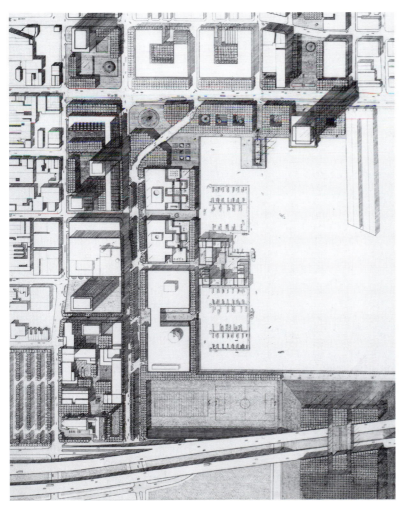

5.4 Baltimore: 1967 Plan.

are experimenting with new uses designed to fill the vacuum left behind in the CBD. In highly developed countries, new uses are selected which will meet the demand created by the new lifestyle of a greatly dispersed population: a great deal more leisure time, divided into ever-smaller increments than in previous generations. (Consider the growth of two-earner families with vacation dates set by unrelated employers, or the sudden switch in Japan from the six-day to the five-day week.)

The new uses that have caught on in the US and increasingly in other developed countries are typified by attractions directed at leisure activities – which appeal both to local residents and to visitors who are more and more mobile, due to increased disposable incomes and the ease of jet air travel or driving on the Interstate with its myriad of comfortable new types of hotels and motels. Market analysts tell us that the leisure audience in the twenty-first century will want more than simply to be entertained; they also want some new knowledge, or understanding, to take away with them – hence the term the "experience economy." This includes such attractions as lifestyle shopping, family entertainment, sports or simulated sports, and cultural venues such as museums, learning centers, art galleries, science centers, and the like.

In addition to providing space for such uses in a central location with a high profile of public recognition, the waterfront also offers a friendly environment for other emerging trends in urban life. Nostalgia is back in favor, and the "new urbanism" or "smart growth" movements, with their emphasis on restoring and infilling old patterns of development, plus the trend toward sustainable development and respect for the environment, all find a natural home in the old city neighborhoods surrounding the port. In addition, there is a strong suspicion that the onslaught of the high-tech world of computers and cyberspace is generating a new form of counter-reaction: a hunger for humane pursuits like reading, or interaction between people. (Perhaps the most popular attraction in Baltimore's Inner Harbor is simply people-watching, from the benches and sidewalk cafés along the Promenade.)

While the new uses favored by the economy and the emerging trends in human preferences seem to favor the waterfront, there is also a trend in technology itself that may make it easier for those demands to be fulfilled. This includes the use of new materials, the adoption (albeit slowly) of new construction methods, including robotics, the availability of onsite and offsite communications technology, and all of the other advances in methodology that are increasing productivity in the development and construction industries.

At the same time there is a universally acknowledged need for the public and private sectors to join as partners in any high-risk, high-profile development undertaking such as a waterfront development project. This has made it possible to create many projects that would have languished for lack of financing in the twentieth century. Government entitlements are issued from the top down. "Gap" financing from the public sector is an accepted necessity. It has been demonstrated that overlapping jurisdictions and territorial rivalries can be minimized by the use of third-party, quasi-public production, or "delivery," systems. Meanwhile, the focusing of responsibility for the waterfront and the prospect of sharing credit for a successful project tend to accelerate the speed of the public sector in reaching planning decisions. A generation of public officials has learned to appreciate the public relations advantages of building a reputation for entrepreneurial skills.

Finally, the list of emerging trends that favor waterfront development must include the overriding globalization of communications, travel, economics and, therefore, tourism. While old ports provide an outstanding vehicle for tourism development, by doing so they also find themselves in a world-wide competition for visitors – after satisfying the local population as the irreducible base. The eyes of both the world and their local constituency will be fixed on them in the years to come.

Waterfront cities at the turn of the Millennium

The opportunity for waterfront development has not been lost on many of the "celebrity" cities in the highly developed world. A list might include such high-profile centers as London, Singapore, Sydney, Buenos Aires, Rotterdam, Honolulu, Chicago, Pittsburgh, New Orleans, Miami, Osaka, Vancouver and Barcelona. Other equally celebrated international cities have lagged behind: one might name Shanghai, Marseilles, Rome, Rio, New York, Los Angeles, Detroit, Hong Kong, Paris, Cairo and Athens. The opportunity is now being approached in most of these cities. It is also on the priority agenda for countless cities in the underdeveloped areas that are emerging onto the global playing field – less well-known cities in Africa, Asia, the Middle East and South America. A steady stream of municipal officials from those nations is visiting the United States to learn from the experience and theories of American professionals on both the public and private sides of the table. A third category might include those cities that have always had an ambient waterfront image, and have never lost it: cities like Venice, Copenhagen, Stockholm, Victoria, Charleston, Quebec, Florence and Amsterdam (in Amsterdam, there are questions being raised about whether there is too much tourism). Finally, for the information of those who are interested in a further pursuit of knowledge on the subject there are the cities which, regardless of their place in history, have emerged as the models for achievement in waterfront development. This might include Baltimore, Boston, San Diego, San Antonio, Cape Town, Toronto, Vancouver and Yokohama, to name just a few in the English-speaking world.

How to meet the challenge

From the experience of a developer who has spent twenty-five years in the implementation of one city's old port development in Baltimore, and another fifteen years advising other cities around the globe on the subject, there are some generic lessons that can be pointed out as instrumental to the success of a waterfront development program. These include:

1 It must be realized that the public and private sectors have common objectives, and can form real public–private partnerships for economic development. This should include an agreement on objectives within

each sector as well as between sectors: e.g., there should be only one entity empowered to take the lead in speaking for the many private sector interests; again, the port and municipality authorities must recognize that their fates are inextricably intertwined.

2   There needs to be a Master Plan of land uses, agreed upon by both sectors. This means a plan that blends the values of both old and new structures and uses, and expresses the desired concept in three dimensions – the only way to achieve a human scale. The plan should provide for public access to and enjoyment of the water (a foreshore, promenade or malecon), with circulation extending from the street grid of the old city, and planned uses of the water as well as the surrounding land. (The view of the skyline from the water may be just as important to the image that is created as the view of the water from the new structures on the land.)

3   There needs to be a realistic Business Plan for the achievement of the concept in the Master Plan based on a realistic projection of market demand and of the availability of public and private funding sources. It should recognize that those sources will be on different timetables, that residential development will probably require some public intervention, that leisure forms of retail development will follow the arrival of people rather than causing it, and that there will probably be a need for some form of "gap" financing for pioneering forms of development.

4   It is important that the plans, and the timetable, have a consensus of support from the community at large. The local population needs to be sold on a concept before it will be embraced by out-of-town developers and investors, and the best way to obtain a sustained community consensus is by making the citizens feel they "own" the project, and the developer is simply the instrument of the public will.

5   Design controls should not be left to the design professionals alone as their priorities are liable to be based on their professional architectural standards, while the public will actually need a project that reflects the implicit values of the local people and their environment. This extends to building sizes, massing, height and proportion, as well as to the aesthetics or good taste reflected in the details. Aerial, or bird's-eye, views are helpful to gain understanding of a three-dimensional plan, but the final test is the view seen by the man or woman in the street, or at water level.

The "delivery system"

The most successful waterfront development projects have been directed in the implementation, or production, phase by the creation of *ad hoc*, quasi-public management systems. These systems come into play after the Vision of the Master Plan has been established through the playing out of the earlier phases:

- the initial intuitive drive for a new image;
- the sorting out of land planning and urban design alternatives;
- public review and reaction to the Plan and, hopefully,
- authorization through the local political process for the government to proceed with implementation of the Plan.

These functions are surrendered or delegated by the government only at the risk of losing touch with the basic objectives of the residents, who will ultimately be the most important customers, or constituents, of the project. They will also elect the officials who must appropriate sufficient up-front capital to build the public infrastructure that will be necessary to attract privately motivated development.

Therefore, the key to a "delivery system" is to have a mechanism that is able to conduct business like a private entity for the sake of speed and efficiency, but which also remains subject to the policy and fiscal control of the publicly elected officials. Such an entity can take many forms, depending on the laws and customs of the locality and the nation involved. In Baltimore, we found the solution in a private, single-purpose, no-stock corporation which contracted to manage the development process as the surrogate of the Mayor and City Council. The contract called for the municipality to pay all of the costs of the corporation's operation, and the corporation to turn any profits over to the municipality.

The corporation was named Charles Center–Inner Harbor Management, Inc., because the Mayor at that time wanted to make sure its purpose was focused strictly on those two projects, and not on creating a larger empire for itself. Put another way, the administrative principle was that the officers of the corporation would have no other thought in their heads when they got out of bed in the morning but to make those projects succeed, in spite of any obstacles that may occur.

The contract with the city gave the corporation a specific list of functions:

- to coordinate (not duplicate) the normal functions of the City Government in the project area: property acquisition, relocation of existing uses, design and construction of infrastructure, and public funding and appropriations;
- to act as spokesman for the plan and the process, creating favorable public relations both locally and externally;
- to recruit developers – private, public or non-profit – who would construct the uses called for by the Master Plan, and to negotiate development agreements with those developers for approval and execution in public by officers of the municipality;
- to review and coordinate the architectural design of all construction, both public and private, to ensure a uniformly high standard of aesthetic quality throughout the projects;
- to control and coordinate the timing of construction, in order to achieve a complementary phasing process and minimize the disruption of other activities;
- to monitor evolving changes in the marketplace and identify changes in the Master Plan as they became indicated.

Obviously, such a public–private contract could be a disaster if it were allowed to run the gauntlet of changing fortunes and factions in local politics. In Baltimore, that was avoided by, first, the designation of respected private, politically neutral executives to head the management corporation, and second, by the early and continuing success of the implementation process, which would have made it very unpopular for any politician to interfere for the wrong reasons.

As a result, the City Government was enabled to act like the private sector in expediting the implementation process without surrendering any of the essential features of the public process. As an added protection, the Maryland state law requires all city bond issues to be approved in a refer- endum of all the voters; so as a practical matter the people had an opportunity every year or two to review the progress to date and decide whether to permit the public funding to continue.

A players' manual

The public and private development professionals who are attracted by the opportunities for waterfront renewal would probably agree that it is no different from other forms of complex, mixed-use development – only more time-consuming, more costly, and therefore more risky and difficult.

More time-consuming because of the lead time required to clear the processes of numerous overlapping jurisdictions (in Baltimore's Inner Harbor, there were fourteen – local, state and federal), plus the added construction time required to create a buildable site, and possibly to reme- diate complex contamination problems, plus the need to phase develop- ment through the early stages when each new venue consisted of a pioneering or untested marketing challenge.

More costly because of the additional construction phase devoted to creating the site, and the hard truth that complex design and leasing chal- lenges require more consultants; that, plus the extended time-frame for development, simply costs more money in terms of carrying costs (since developers use borrowed money, they have to pay interest over the entire process).

More risky because more often than not the development program is unique and untested, and that dictates a gradual phasing and build-up process, which allows time for the business cycle to shift and alter the cost and income projections, or for a change in public tastes to demand a dif- ferent merchandising mix. The sturdy souls who are still determined to take on the challenge of waterfront development (and the romance and sheer adventure of the vision attracts many who will) would do well to understand the new elements involved: the emerging new uses of the CBD, the emphasis on environment or sustainability, the increasing role of the market for lifestyle product and humanism as a counterpoint to technology, and finally – and most important – the need to perform in the arena of global competition.

It is no longer enough for private sector players to calculate the risks and determine the mix and timing of a mixed-use development at the water- front. Both public and private sectors need to understand the need for obtaining enforceable site control, pre-development "front money" and commitments of public funding and entitlements before promising to deliver a certain development product. (More often than not, because of the previous history of the site, the first capital invested will need to be the public sector's share.) They must appreciate the all-powerful challenge of the supply–demand equation: project cost/benefit ratios, the need for market support of privately financed uses (how many people will come, and how much they will spend per capita); the different rhythms of funding availability in the public and private sectors, and of course the risk of business cycles upsetting any or all of the assumptions. All of these factors dictate a need to remain flexible in implementation while adhering faithfully to the vision, or the principles, in the Master Plan that the people have adopted as their own.

In sum, the players will need to understand that the stakes are high – both for winning or losing – because the waterfront is probably the only one the community has, and they'd better be prepared to do it right because they won't be given another chance.

6 New millennium Bilbao

Alfonso Vegara

The city of Bilbao is currently enjoying a greatly enhanced urban image since the Guggenheim Museum opened a few years ago. However, the metropolitan area of the city has been undergoing an urban transformation less heralded but no less dramatic. The roots of this transformation lie in the reconceptualization of the entire Basque Country as a European "city-region," as outlined in the Basque regional strategy developed in the 1990s. The Nervión River, at the heart of the metropolitan area, instead of remaining a physical and social barrier, will become the axis of urban redevelopment for the city-region seeking to face the challenges of the new millennium.

The regional vision of the Basque Country

The Basque Autonomous Community, or the Basque Country, consists of the three provinces of Bizkaia, Guípuzcoa and Alava. The Basque Country enjoys an important self-government headed by the Basque Parliament, located in the Basque capital city of Vitoria-Gasteiz. The Basque Country has its own police force and a distinct tax system managed by the Territorial Treasuries.

The Basque Country is the first autonomous community in Spain to have a regional planning strategy approved by its regional parliament. The "Directrices de Ordenación Territorial" (DOT), or the "Regional Planning Guidelines," is the planning instrument which has the capacity to coordinate the sectoral policies and the urban plans that affect the 250 or so municipalities that comprise the Basque Autonomous Community. The DOT was developed from 1990 and formally adopted in 1997 by the Basque Government.

The basic idea behind the regional planning strategy of the Basque Country is the reconceptualization of the Basque Country as a European "city-region" that will constitute a single job market. As a city-region, the Basque Country would be better positioned to avoid urban sprawl, balance the urban system, and maintain the urban identity of cities, towns and villages.

The Basque city-region sits on the frontier between the older industrial-

6.1 Connecting the Atlantic and Mediterranean arcs.

ized European regions and the European regions evolving new industrial structures. It is also located at the intersection of the Paris–Madrid axis and the Ebro Valley–northern Spain corridor. The Basque Country is therefore extremely well located as a "hinge-point" to lead the process of connecting the Atlantic Arc with the Mediterranean Arc through the Ebro Axis, which is one of the most dynamic in the Spanish economy.

The city-region has a surface area roughly that of the metropolitan area of a city like Miami or Sydney. With a population of some 2 million inhabitants, the reconceptualization of the Basque Country as a city-region is critical to its efforts to be relevant and competitive in the global economy.

The key points of the Basque regional strategy are:

1 *Creating a system of complementary capitals*. The three largest Basque cities – Bilbao, Donostia-San Sebastian and Vitoria-Gasteiz – are almost perfectly distributed in the region. The distances between the three cities are short, and each city clearly has its own function and personality. Bilbao is the economic and financial center, Donostia-San Sebastian is the elegant capital of culture and tourism, while Vitoria-Gasteiz is the political and administrative capital.

   The challenge is to identify and strengthen the mutual complementarities of each urban node, interconnecting them with essential and modern infrastructure systems, such as the proposed Basque "Y" of the High-Speed Rail system. The system of complementary capitals will build a solid interrelationship while maintaining their distinctive urban profiles.

2 *Renewing the roles of the Basque network of medium-sized cities*. The

6.2 Bilbao: a European hingepoint.

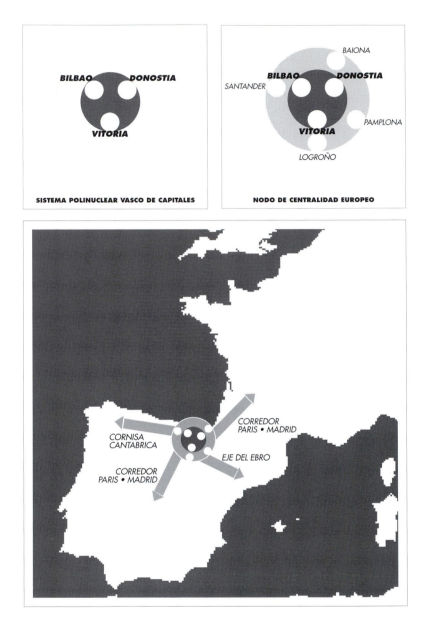

SISTEMA POLINUCLEAR VASCO DE CAPITALES

NODO DE CENTRALIDAD EUROPEO

fifteen or so medium-sized Basque cities that lead the "Functional Areas," or the intermediate regions within the provinces, are important nodes necessary for the integration of the urban and the rural. Their role is not only in maintaining this delicate territorial balance, but also in maintaining the social balance through the strong feeling of ownership of its citizens, and in the balance among places of residence, work and leisure.

These medium-sized cities are facing the challenges by improving their urban quality and their integration with the environment. The urban decline will need to be stemmed, their economic base strengthened and greater links for cooperation and exchange established.

3 *Revaluing the system of rural nuclei with connections to the natural*

areas. The Basque Country has more than 160 villages and historical centers that have maintained their identity, morphology and image. Almost perfectly integrated in their environment, these towns and villages enrich the landscape of the city-region. Collectively, they are an enormous cultural heritage, as well as a potential competitive advantage for the region.

These rural nuclei are essential for the survival of Basque traditions and idiosyncrasies, but as a network they can have significance only within the context of the Basque city-region. About a hundred of these villages contain the second residences of families that live in the principal Basque cities. The rural towns and villages will be the basis of the emerging rural tourism that could be vital for the future of these spaces.

4 *An alternative to urban sprawl*. A key concept of the Basque regional strategy is the prohibition of new development outside of the existing urban and rural nuclei. This restriction protects the natural landscape from sprawl while safeguarding the coherent identity of the urban and rural nuclei.

It is for this alternative to urban sprawl that the Basque regional strategy was awarded an Urban and Regional Planning Prize in 1995, given by the European Commission and the European Council of Town Planners.

5 *Creating a network of natural spaces and ecological corridors*. The Basque Country is a region of great physical and climatic diversity. From rugged northern coastlines and mountains, to the Mediterranean plains and the Atlantic valleys, these spaces are not only closely interlaced with, but have helped shape the development of, the urban system. These spaces are invaluable ecological and visual assets that maintain the natural biodiversity and the quality of the landscape, as well as provide many leisure options.

The restrictions of urban sprawl have protected these natural spaces and corridors from future urban intrusion. However, these natural assets need to be linked together into a coherent network, as well as linked to the urban system that will allow them to be better enjoyed and managed.

6 *Connecting the Basque city-region to important neighboring cities*. To develop the natural strategic role as a European "hinge-point," stronger connections need to be established with neighboring cities such as Santander, Logroño, Pamplona, and Bayonne, as well as with the larger European urban system. This has clear implications for the development of the road and high-speed rail network, as well as for airport and seaport development. A competitive role in certain sectors – logistics and tourism, for instance – will be dependent on the connectivity of the Basque city-region.

The "Miracle of Bilbao" can only be understood in the context of a society that has strong regional sensibilities and a sense of identity. The Basque society has drawn up for itself a very efficient new system of planning that allows for working at the regional scale, at the intermediate scale, at the scale of the municipalities, and at the scale of specific projects.

The concept of the Basque Country as a city-region is a new frame of action that allows the integration of all the urban and natural assets, and to participate in a global economy with a clear vision of the competitive advantages as a city-region. By taking such a regional perspective, the Basque Government was able to identify a set of high-priority actions to renew its cities and its obsolete urban areas.

Metropolitan Bilbao: the river as an axis of urban redevelopment

From the beginning of this century, an increasing amount of industry and inhabitants have located themselves along the banks of the River Nervión. Today, while the municipality of Bilbao only has about 400,000 inhabitants, Metropolitan Bilbao comprises more than twenty municipalities and has nearly one million inhabitants.

The population density of the Metropolitan Area of Bilbao is nearly 2,000 persons per square kilometer, and it is in this area that almost half of the population and the economic activity of the entire Basque Country are located. In many respects, the success or failure of the Basque Country depends on the success or failure of Metropolitan Bilbao.

The waterfront has featured prominently in the growth and development of the city since its foundation in the year 1300. However, the industrial development in the past two centuries has converted the river into a great physical and psychological barrier. The Nervión River has come to represent both the physical and social division of the metropolitan region. Historically, the principal port facilities and shipyards were located almost to the heart of the city. Since the ships needed to reach these facilities, low-level or pedestrian bridges connecting the two sides of the river could not be built.

Demographically, the wealthier families and the families with Basque origins have generally located on the right bank of the river. These are families who are able to speak the Basque language, and have traditionally voted for Nationalist or right-wing parties. The more important universities have also been founded on the right bank.

The principal industrial facilities are located in the municipalities on the left bank of the river. Many immigrants from the other regions in Spain came to look for work in the Basque economy, especially during the 1960s and the 1970s. The people who live and work here are lower-income families who only speak Spanish. They have generally not integrated very well with the existing Basque society, and have traditionally voted for the parties to the left of the political spectrum.

In this way, the economic model established the physical and social segregation of the city-region. However, the model itself was clearly obsolete by the end of the 1970s and during the 1980s, leading to a prolonged economic crisis in the region. The obsolete riverfront facilities were allowed to decay, and the newer urban development turned its back to the river.

It is in this context that the regional strategy of the Basque Country considered the renovation and the rehabilitation of the river and its surroundings to be the highest priority. The principal idea is to transform the waterfronts from brownfields, that are physically and economically obsolete, into a renewed area to reconstruct a Bilbao for the next century from the ruins of an industrial past.

Instead of remaining a physical and social barrier, the Nervión River would become an axis for the social and urban reintegration of the metropolitan area. Among the strategies that have been adopted include:

- The extension of the Port of Bilbao, the first phase of which was completed in November 1998, is a key component for the economic regeneration of the region. The relocating of the old port facilities situated along the river to modern, consolidated ones closer to the sea, was also a major step that finally allowed the building of low-level bridges that will physically connect both banks of the Nervión.
- The ambitious program of cleaning the river, eliminating the industrial ruins, decontaminating the brownfields, and, above all, providing new infrastructure to improve access to the area such as new urban roads, the Metro, airport improvements, railway access, port and logistic facilities, and so on.
- Placing new uses on the newly vacated areas and in old industrial buildings. These new uses include cultural and educational facilities, technology and science parks, commercial and government offices, support services, green and leisure space, and also housing. In short, the most sophisticated facilities and the economic activities that will be leading the Basque economy in the new century will be located next to the river of Bilbao.

Accomplishments and projects for the future

A number of specific projects have also been developed in recent years. These projects represent the beginnings of the ambitious urban renewal program of Bilbao.

The Bilbao Guggenheim Museum

The Guggenheim Museum is perhaps the most emblematic of these projects. The waterfront location of the museum, at one end of the Abandoibarra district, below an existing bridge and next to a railway line, was one of the most degraded spaces in the city. The Museum has quickly become a symbol of the renovation of Bilbao, and an international symbol of the innovative vocation of the Basque society as it meets the challenges of the new millennium.

The impact of the Museum on the local economy has been extraordinary. Before the Museum was built, the weekend occupation rate of the hotels in the city was only about 20 percent. Today, it is practically impossible to find a room during the weekends. Some international hotel chains have also begun to develop new hotels.

Some of the local engineering and equipment companies, and others that participated in the construction of the building (which has a steel structure, titanium façade, and stone cladding), are finding new, global markets on the basis of the international publicity provided by the Museum.

The Bilbao Metro

The Metro system of Bilbao was one of the first acts of urban renovation in the city. Norman Foster, the well-known British architect, designed the system. The distinctive stations are predominantly constructed of glass, stainless steel and concrete, and project an image of modernity, innovation and excellence. The Metro was inaugurated in 1995, and offers an efficient public transport service in the metropolitan area of Bilbao, carrying more than 50 million passengers in 1999.

The Metro system is currently being extended, and a new line being added. The technology used in the tunnels that cross beneath the Nervión is being applied by Basque companies in other places around the world.

The Palacio Euskalduna Conference and Music Center

The Palacio Euskalduna is a huge complex containing a conference center and an auditorium; it is also the home of the symphony orchestra. The building was designed to symbolize a large ship, and is located in the opposite end of the Abandoibarra riverside area across from the Guggenheim Museum. This area, until very recently, was the location of one of the main shipyards in Bilbao.

The new Sondika airport

The Bilbao Sondika airport is being developed as the premier passenger gateway to the Basque Country, while the airport at Vitoria-Gasteiz has the complementary vocation as the cargo and logistics gateway.

The airport is completing an ambitious expansion to double its current capacity. The existing terminal handled 2.2 million passengers in 1999. The new airport complex has been designed by the well-known Spanish architect Santiago Calatrava, and is about to be officially opened. The distinctive designs for the new terminal building and the new control tower have become known as the "dove" and the "falcon" respectively.

6.3 The Palacio Euskalduna, Bilbao.

Historic heart of Bilbao

The historic center of Bilbao is also undergoing a dramatic change. Many traditional buildings, such as the Arriaga Theatre, the "Seven Streets," the old railway station and covered market are undergoing extensive rehabilitation. The spillover effect from the interest generated by the Guggenheim has had a very positive impact, and the historic heart of Bilbao is discovering a new role as a complementary attraction to the museum.

Nervión River projects

A number of urban design projects are also being developed to organize the spaces along the riverfront. Most of these projects are only proposals at this stage, but they reveal the high levels of ambition and the tremendous urban opportunities that will emerge along the edges of the Nervión in the near future.

These projects try to address some of the key issues along the river, such as the design of physical connections to bridge the river; the urban design of the new Zorrozaurre island; the area around the Rontegi bridge; and the confluence of the Nervión and its tributary, the Cadagua, downstream.

As an urban renovation and rehabilitation axis the Nervión is, without doubt, a huge waterfront regeneration project that will take at least twenty-five years to complete.

The miracle of Bilbao

Like so many other European areas affected by the decline of traditional industries, Bilbao also witnessed an alarming decline in urban conditions, especially in the 1980s. This decline was partly due to industrial and economic obsolescence, and the lack of competitiveness of the local companies and industries. As a result, unemployment levels rose while the relative standards of living fell. Extremely high levels of pollution accompanied the loss of urban identity. Social and political problems were also aggravated by the economic situation.

In the last decade of the twentieth century Bilbao has chosen to pursue a new economic and urban profile, and to achieve a real integration with the global economy and the global world. Some people have called this transformation the beginning of the "miracle" of Bilbao.

Although there is clearly still a long way to go, there are a number of reasons why a "New Millennium Bilbao" could arise from the ruins of an old industrial past:

- *Political will and cooperation*. The different levels of administration – town halls, provincial government, Basque regional government, and the central government of Spain – have been able to exhibit real political will and cooperation in the pursuit of common aims. The Basque Country has a tradition of cooperation. The ability to cooperate is a key competitive advantage for the region.
- *New regional planning strategy*. The planning instrument, "Directrices de Ordenación Territorial" (DOT), or the "Regional Planning Guidelines," that was formally adopted in 1997, places Bilbao within the

context of not only its metropolitan area but also within the strategic regional planning of the entire Basque Country.

- *Citizen participation and support.* Bilbao also enjoys the full and active support of the local business community for the recovery of the city. In fact, there has been the successful creation of a number of dynamic public and private partnerships, such as the "Bilbao Metropoli 30" and the "Bilbao Ría 2000."
- *Successful pilot projects.* The importance of the successful initial projects cannot be overestimated. These initial experiences, such as the treatment of old industrial sites, the recovery of the historical center, the Metro system, the Guggenheim Museum, the Opera House and Convention Center, the new airport, and the extension of the Port of Bilbao, etc., have generated tremendous local, national and international publicity.

However, these changes that I have described in the city are only the surface changes. The greatest miracle that Bilbao is experiencing is a dramatic change in attitude. The feelings of failure and pessimism brought about by prolonged economic crisis and political conflicts have given way to a collective optimism in Bilbao and the Basque society as a whole. The majority of the Basque community – the public institutions, the private sector, and the civil society – is now convinced that it is indeed possible to reinvent Bilbao and the Basque Country in the new post-industrial age. This is the true miracle of Bilbao.

PART IV
PORT AND CITY RELATIONS

7 Modern ports and historic cities
Genoa and Las Palmas de Gran Canaria

Richard Marshall

Recent decades have witnessed substantial changes in the relationships between ports and cities and between cities, ports, and the regions in which they are located. With changes in the nature of port operations and infrastructure, there has been a wide trend of ports shifting to deepwater locations in order to maintain their competitive advantage. Such moves have caused major changes in the relationships between ports and urban areas and have impacted the environments of coastal zones as well. Once ports were looked at in isolation; now they are seen as one part of larger urban systems and larger transportation infrastructures. This is of critical importance for planners and architects in thinking of ways to develop spatial strategies that will advance a city's economic potential. Such considerations require a balance between the agenda of port operations and those of the urban situation, and these are often in conflict with each other.

7.1 View of containers, Genoa.

Historically the administrative functions of modern ports and cities were completely separate. Decisions made by one were without consideration of the other. Although historically not the case, the boundary between port and city is often a contested one. Overlapping zones are the battleground of modern planning in many cities. Often ports fear that urban development, particularly luxury waterfront housing, will influence and ultimately restrict essential port operations. Likewise, cities fear that an increase in port business will create more traffic and noise in residential areas.

The port cities of Genoa and Las Palmas de Gran Canaria provide two examples where these conflicts continue to influence both the politics of urban development and the form of the city. Genoa is an example of enlightened relationships between the Port Authority and the municipality. Las Palmas is somewhat more typical. Both, however, shed light on the nature of this relationship and the importance of it in shaping the urban condition. Of particular relevance is the influence such a relationship has on the physical construction of the city and how the zone of overlap and conflict is managed.

The New Genoa Port Master Plan is an innovative document. Its objective is not just to describe a list of "maritime works" to increase port facilities; rather, for the first time, it is to develop a plan capable of establishing a communication link between the port and the city. The new Port Master Plan is intended to envision a new pattern of development for the city of Genoa, one where both agencies influence the outcome. This document emphasizes a common planning intention and aims not at a mediated interface between the two but toward a new condition where both port and city combine to create a new zone leading to an urban experience of unprecedented quality.

The planning of the waterfront in Las Palmas is more typical in that it is jurisdictionally fragmented. Numerous public agencies control the waterfront and have responsibility for various aspects of its spatial organization. In response to the disjointed nature of this situation, the Port Authorities of Las Palmas combined resources to rethink the stretch of waterfront between Barranco Guiniguada and Santa Catalina. The result was a consultant's report that represents the current thinking of urban and port development in the city. The Port Authority in Las Palmas has also sponsored a Harvard Design School studio, under the direction of Dean Peter Rowe, in order to obtain ideas for what the future of this territory may be.

The Genoa context

Genoa is a port city of about one million people on the northwest coast of Italy. It is the center of the Province of Liguria and one of the leading trade cities in the Mediterranean. Sandwiched between the Ligurian Mountains and the sea, it overlooks the Mare Ligure and the harbor. Its old port, shaped in a large arc, is situated in front of the historic center of the city – one of the most distinguished and extensive in Europe. The city extends along a 20-mile-long coastline, of which 15 miles are devoted to port activities, the Airport, and the Fiera Exhibition Center. The Genoa International Airport, Cristoforo Colombo, is located seven miles from the city center. This facility handled approximately 950,000 passengers in 1998.

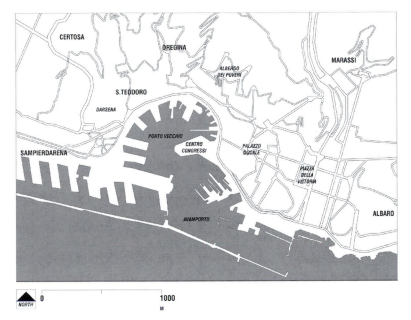

The port of Genoa is the seventh busiest in Europe and first in the Mediterranean in terms of traffic volume. In 1997, the port handled a total of 1.2 million TEU of containers and 2.4 million passengers through its twenty-five terminals.

Genoa is ideally located for commercial trade activities in Europe with an efficient road system to France, through the Tyrrhenian corridor to the north, plus a reliable railroad network linking it with the Po Valley and the rest of Europe. Plans exist to build a third mountain pass with a high-speed train line to improve connections with Milan, and an additional line to France.

Genoa is a polycentric city. In the middle of the urban area, in direct contact with the old port, lies the historic center. A newer nineteenth-century center lies outside of the historic core. An industrial city for more than a century, with a strong public sector, and the leading port in the Mediterranean for cargo and passenger traffic, Genoa has undergone profound changes over the last ten years. It has gone from being an industrial city to one that accommodates modern tertiary services as well as small to medium-sized companies, many of which operate in the computer, electronic and telecommunication sectors. Genoa has also invested heavily in culture and tourism and in the construction of new and remodeled hotels. This redevelopment initiative has also enhanced the value of monuments and important historic buildings as well as the urban environment and public parks. One of these projects, the City of Children, dedicated to the youngest residents of Genoa, lies within the old port. In terms of the quality of initiatives and the number of visitors, this project has already surpassed its model, the "Cité des Infants" in Paris.

Genoa is the first Italian city to have a Port Master Plan that, together with the city's General Master Plan, has made it possible to develop urban and strategic planning for the near future. Many abandoned areas are now undergoing redevelopment, redesign and reuse as new business sites

7.3 Bacino Porto Vecchio, Genoa.

or mass distribution centers. Genoa is playing an increasingly important role in and between the Mediterranean and other geopolitical areas, through trade and alliances. One of the most important is the cooperation agreement signed with Athens and Barcelona for 2004. At this time, Genoa will be the European City of Culture, Athens the site of the Olympic Games, and Barcelona the center of an important UNESCO initiative.

Genoa has a remarkable history. Established in Roman times, near the site of the present-day berthing structures, the township grew in the Middle Ages and settled into the coastal arc, which subsequently supported the first port and commercial uses. The town was an independent municipality in the eleventh century, established as an oligarchy republic. City life focused on maritime traffic and a powerful and rich noble class emerged, which governed and controlled the city's urban structure. The Genoese economy, linked to the sea, gave rise to an extensive seafaring culture. In fact, the Genoese were among the most important navigators of the period and were involved in some of the most important geographic discoveries. Columbus obviously heads the list. Thus, Genoa became one of the richest and most influential port cities in Europe. It was able to maintain its independence because of its great financial power, created as a result of cash loans and fleets chartered to the greatest European kingdoms.

With Genoa's increasing wealth, the city transformed from a township into a city. Palatial buildings often hosted visiting diplomats and monarchs. Parts of these still exist and are now under renovation. By the twelfth century, the curving stretch of the Ripa developed. During the thirteenth century, the port expanded with the construction of important operating structures, including the Darsena (dockyard), the Arsenale (navy yard), the Commenda, dry docks and new berths. These linked to the trade and commercial activities in the Ripa, at the water's edge. Stone quays were constructed to enclose the Mandraccio (inner harbor) and the Molo

7.4 Inside the old port, Genoa.

Vecchio (old wharf). Genoa had a working waterfront where trade and commercial activities came together. Deals were made under the Ripa's arcades. Tall brick warehouses spread around the harbor, directly overlooking the landing stages, and were equipped with *logge* and *embroli* for storing goods. The appearance of the port, formed during the twelfth and thirteenth centuries, remained substantially unchanged from then to the industrial expansions of the nineteenth century. Due to a private donation, a reconfiguration occurred in the nineteenth century and the commercial and working aspects of the port became separated. The industrial harbor, constructed with new berths and warehouses, became functionally and physically separated from the city by fences and rail tracks as the port and the city industrialized.

Beginning in the nineteenth century, a new inland urban center, with residential areas extending into the nearby hills, emerged from the city's ancient walls. During the twentieth century, the local residents abandoned the historic center in favor of newer accommodation. The city expanded, encompassing the districts to the west and east, while the creation of new, large industrial structures and urban services led to extensive urbanization of the Pocevera and Bisagno Valleys perpendicular to the new coastline.

The industrial port shifted gradually to the west at the beginning of the twentieth century. With the advent of containerization, this expansion included the construction of new structures built to handle cargo. This, in turn, led to the abandonment of the historic port facing the old city. Like many cities around the world, this led to a crisis in the industrial sector, once the driving force of the city's economy. In response, the public administration began a complex and ambitious plan to redesign the waterfront, establishing important tourism activities and services for the city.

Throughout its history, Genoa has gone through alternating periods of great prosperity and profound crisis. After each crisis, the city has changed radically in terms of its economic structure and social organization. These shifts correspond to significant transformations in its image and urban structure. In the Middle Ages the city was a booming trade port. Between the sixteenth and seventeenth centuries it lost control of cargo traffic, only to emerge as Europe's main financial center. In the nineteenth century, the port rediscovered its role and because of this the city took an active part in establishing the Kingdom of Italy, becoming the center for nationalized heavy industry – steel, mechanics, and shipbuilding.

The world-wide restructuring of industry, the conversion of maritime transport modes, and the crisis in the system of state shareholdings in the industry represented a global challenge for Genoa. The start of the 1990s produced the first results of this transformation with an increase in port traffic after years of decline. It also brought the realization of initiatives to reutilize industrial areas and the first positive responses to efforts to launch tourism in a city. Genoa has the advantage of being able to rely on its position within a very important environmental area, on its extensive artistic heritage, and on possessing one of Europe's largest historic centers.

The factors behind the economic recovery of the city include the increase in demand for air transport, the significant development of port activities (in particular cruise ships), and a rediscovered penchant for conference and tourism initiatives. The increase in port activity lies significantly in the area of container traffic. The main Mediterranean ports have developed quickly over the last five years with an average growth rate of 19 percent compared to about 8 percent for North Europe. The Italian ports enjoyed growth of about 21 percent. Ports with the best overall performance during the last five years, measured in terms of their average growth rates, were Genoa (+30 percent), Valencia (+21 percent), and Barcelona (+16.5 percent) (Port Authority of Genoa, 1999).

Genoa has thirteen 4-star and twenty-eight 3-star hotels. The city also has a Conference Center and numerous other convention sites. It hosts important trade fairs, including the Boat Show, Euroflora, and cultural events such as the N. Paganini International Violin Award. The port of Genoa processed a total of 1,265,593 TEU of container traffic and 80,060 passengers in 1998 (Autorità Portuale di Genova, 1999).

The Las Palmas de Gran Canaria context

The Port of Las Palmas de Gran Canaria is one of the most important in Spain. In comparison to Genoa, the Puerto de Las Palmas handled 484,477 TEU of container traffic and 907,456 passengers in 1998 (Puertos de Las Palmas, 1999). For five centuries, it has been a base for ships sailing on the mid-Atlantic. Its strategic location and the excellent condition of its bay made it one of the most important ports in the main sea routes between Europe, Africa and America. Christopher Columbus used its bay to prepare and repair the caravels *La Pinta* and *La Niña* during his first voyage to America in 1492.

Las Palmas de Gran Canaria is the capital of the province of Las Palmas and is located on the northeast of the island of Gran Canaria. The population of the city is 395,000 distributed over an area of some 40 square miles. Las Palmas is the most densely populated city in the Canary Islands

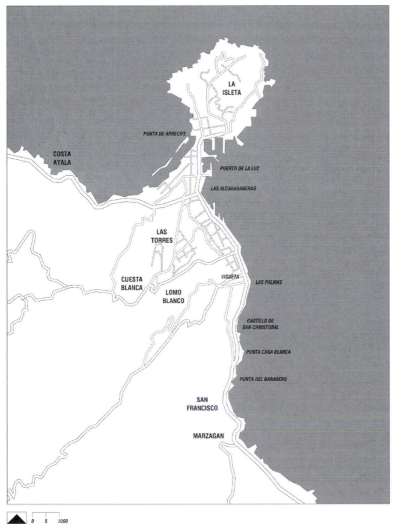

7.5 Map of Las Palmas waterfront.

and the seventh densest in Spain. The Canaries consist of seven islands: El Hierro, La Gomera, Tenerife, Gran Canaria, Lanzarote and Fuerteventura. Two provinces make up the islands: Santa Cruz de Tenerife is the western capital and Las Palmas de Gran Canaria is the eastern capital. The city of Las Palmas occupies a magnificent isthmus formed by two bays. On the western side lies Playa de las Canteras and on the eastern edge lies Playa de las Alcaravaneras, which is the home of the port. The topography of Gran Canaria is undulating, evidence of the volcanic origins of the island. Craters and cones serve as reminders of the geologic past of the region. Many *barrancos*, or narrow valleys, cover the island and determine the form of development in the urban areas.

The city of Las Palmas de Gran Canaria was founded in 1478, by invading Spanish forces, at the mouth of the Barranco de Guiniguada, which is the site of the historic center, Vegueta. The original inhabitants of the island were the Guanches, thought to have been of Berber origin. Until the arrival of the Europeans, the Canary culture was Neolithic and many

7.6 View from Las Torres, Las Palmas.

archeological sites exist today. The mouth of the Barranco de Guiniguada was the only part of the city to be urbanized until the middle of the nineteenth century. Until then, the city remained within the limit of walls. In 1881, work began on the Puerto de La Luz at the southeast end of La Isleta and a new population center soon developed. An esplanade covers the site of the original port at Triana, which occurred with the construction of the Ciudad del Mar in the 1960s.

The growing importance of the port led to the construction of more wharves and the area around the port developed, producing a new city center. Between 1925 and 1950, the two urban centers grew toward each other. The edge of the waterfront soon developed as the port esplanades began to take over the coastline. Land was reclaimed to increase the depths of moorings and to construct the water's edge. During the 1960s and 1970s, the two centers continued to grow together, eventually filling in the valleys that cut the escarpment. Today the city is undertaking a major revitalization. Of critical importance is the improvement in city infrastructure. A new ring road and various highways, under construction, are intended to improve communication with the rest of the island. The intention of these improvements is to improve the "urban quality" of Las Palmas, including such things as parks, beaches, sporting and cultural facilities.

Since 1852, the Port of Las Palmas has been a Free Port. In the 1960s, tourism became a significant revenue generator for Las Palmas and gradually changed the social and economic structure of the Canaries. Since the 1960s, Las Palmas has become the commercial and cultural center of Gran Canaria. Until the nineteenth century, agriculture was the fundamental base of the economy of Gran Canaria. During the second half of the twentieth century the ports, trade and commerce, tourism, and the export of agricultural produce underwent spectacular growth. The Canary Islands have traditionally been granted a special and specific fiscal and economic regime – known as "Regimen Economico y Fiscal" (REF). The REF contains a series of fiscal incentives aimed at the creation and development of entrepreneurial activities to make Gran Canaria attractive for investment. Companies established in the islands are eligible for a series of benefits, grants and subsidies. Gran Canaria is also eligible for a series of incentives for business activities granted by the European Union, the State Government and the Regional Government, which complement other support that businesses receive through the REF. In addition, Gran Canaria is also included in the zones of Objective 1 of the European Union, allowing preferential access to European Structural Funds.

The free trade status of the Canary Islands reflects in exemptions to consumers, lower indirect tax rates, and the avoidance of certain state monopolies. The Special Economic and Tax Regime for the Canaries (Spanish: REF) was implemented in 1972. This aimed at promoting the economic and social development of the Archipelago. When Spain joined the European Community in 1985, the Special Economic and Tax Regime for the Canaries changed to fit with national and European conditions. The Department of Economic Affairs and Treasury authorized the Free Trade Zone (FTZ) in 1998. The aim of the FTZ is to become an inward processing area to promote exports, thus encouraging the establishment of trade and industrial activities in the Canaries.

The Free Trade Zone of Gran Canaria is located in two different strategic areas, the Port of Las Palmas and the Arinaga Industrial Zone. The Port of Las Palmas serves as a strategic export point to Europe, Africa and the Atlantic coast of Latin America. The Arinaga Industrial Estate is located in the area with the greatest industrial and trade potential on the island, just thirteen miles from the most important tourist resort in the Canarian Archipelago and five miles from the Airport. The Free Trade Zone in the

7.7 View over the Playa de las Canteras, Las Palmas.

Port of Las Palmas provides 500,000 square feet of completely built-up surface in the Península del Nido, available for any company devoted to the production, transformation, handling or trading of goods. The Arinaga Industrial Zone is one of the biggest industrial areas in Spain, covering a surface of 48 million square feet. Of this, some 20 million square feet are set aside for industrial activities. The rest of this area is devoted to equipment, and residential areas (The Las Palmas Chamber of Commerce, Industry and Shipping, 1999).

Defining a new waterfront in Genoa

The redevelopment of the Genoese waterfront began with a series of major projects carried out to celebrate the 500th anniversary of the discovery of America in 1992. The International Expo held in the area of the old port included the cotton warehouses built in 1910 and the entire area of the Free Port. Renzo Piano developed the overall plan, which included the renovation of historic buildings and the construction of the Convention Center and the Aquarium. Today, the area is a public cultural space. In addition to the Aquarium there are bars and restaurants, shops, a multiple theater cinema complex, a children's library, the "City of Children," and the Sea and Navigation Museum. A residential and hotel development is under construction immediately west of the area on the Calvi and Morosini wharves.

To the west is the municipal Darsena, which is the subject of a special project for which a portion is already completed. The municipal Darsena, located on the waterfront of the historic center, includes an array of buildings with their corresponding water expanse that originated from the ancient core of the dockyard serving the port. With the decline in the port as a trading center, the University Faculty of Economics and Commerce relocated into the Scio area. The transformation of the Darsena is ongoing, related to the development of the entire historic port.

The municipality has some definite objectives for the area. These include urban and environmental redevelopment with new and complementary activities that support the University's activities and its integration into the bordering Galata area. In addition, there are improvements to public space and the infrastructure, and the landscaping of the vehicular and pedestrian ways, with particular attention on the link to the Prè, an undergound pedestrian crossing under via Gramsci and the Darsena subway. This improvement includes the Cembalo and Bacinetto areas, the demolition of the Famagosta area up to the level of the adjacent water treatment system, and the recovery of about a hundred parking spaces which are in addition to the 180 spaces currently available on the roof. In addition, the municipality aims to develop new functions in the Darsena, including a high school, by redeveloping existing buildings. These redevelopment ideas include the Tabarca area, with the possible relocation of compatible activities from the outlying areas and the inclusion of technology systems to serve the historic center.

Another University department entering the Darsena is the Faculty of Engineering. Plans call for the renovation of the Hennebique building and the Customs building to provide approximately 700,000 square feet of space. This effort aims at establishing a model in Europe to define other historic adaptations. The introduction of a massive public service facility will revitalize the economy of the area and attract new businesses, bars, restaurants and, it is hoped, new residential development.

The Ponte Parodi Conversion involves the construction of a large center in the heart of the historic port. Located in the center of the Genoese arc, it is the only modern pier projecting into the port basin. The plan calls for the construction of a large public square facing the sea, focusing on leisure and cultural activities. An international architectural competition will be held for the site with the intention of creating a building and space that projects an internationally recognizable image of the city. The New Ferry Terminal in the San Benigno Administrative Center includes a multifunctional building for transiting passengers, with business services, bars and restaurants, travel agencies, and offices. The terminal will accommodate 2.5 million passengers, 700,000 cars, and approximately 110,000 trucks each year.

The new Genoa Port Master Plan

The revitalization of the waterfront in Genoa is a massive undertaking. The new Port Master Plan for Genoa summarizes the intentions of the city and the port and is a remarkable document. The formal adoption of the Master Plan, in 2000, by the Port Committee establishes a productive relationship between the port and the city for the first time. The Master Plan aims to contribute toward a new pattern of development in the city, one that

7.8 Old wharves, Genoa.

denies the segregation of the city from the port and instead adopts an inclusive position where both contribute to the physical and programmatic outcome.

The old port plan dates to 1964. This plan was typical for its day and involved maritime harbor works without any consideration for the city. In fact the 1964 plan promoted port expansion at the expense of the urban fabric and involved a major appropriation of waterfront between Prà and Voltri. The 1964 plan was based, erroneously, on the idea that Genoa would not only maintain its port role in the Mediterranean but would improve upon it. The rationalization of industrial and port infrastructure in the 1970s shifted shipping activity away from the Mediterranean basin. The northern European ports grew in influence and Genoa's port fell into decline and eventually decay. The redefinition of port use on the waterfront brought with it a concomitant appreciation for the ancient waterfront. This new attitude accepted the idea of the waterfront as part of an ancient town center. During the 1980s, the town appropriated parts of the industrial waterfront in the Ripa and removed barriers (customs, railway, road) between the port and the city. This revitalized the connections between the ancient core and the water.

In a remarkable reversal of fortune, the 1990s saw Genoa gain the port volume that it had lost over the previous twenty-year period. Because of this, the pressure between the space requirements of the port and the city were again brought into conflict and required the rethinking of port and city relations. Unlike the port plan of 1964, however, this new period of port activity brought with it a new attitude toward conflict resolution between the port and the city. The "Intensa con il Comune" is a policy that defines this new relationship between port and city and outlays a procedure of discussions prior to the adoption of the Port Master Plan. These include obtaining the opinion of the Consiglio Superiore dei Lavori Publici, procedures for evaluating the environmental impact, and the overview of the Regione. The Regione reviews and approves the final plan.

In 1996, the development of the Port Master Plan began, the same year as the municipality of Genoa launched the new General Town Planning Scheme. These plans present a unique occurrence that are evidence of a recovered dialogue to overcome long-standing feuds over territorial occupation. The collaborative process is worthy of elaboration. For much of the history of industrial activity in Genoa, the municipality and the port have had a strained relationship. The establishment of a "cultural process," which includes a variety of other players, made the task of establishing a common ground easier. The University of Genoa played an important role in the formation, which led to the creation of the Port Authority Plan Agency. This Agency includes academic staff, researchers, scholars and students. The Plan Agency also collaborates with consultants, including Rem Koolhaas and OMA, Marcel Smets, and Manuel de Solà Morales. The Agency conducts conferences to explore useful comparisons with other planning schemes. The Agency also meets with the Assoindustria (Industrial Operators Association and the Port Operators Association), the Chamber of Commerce, the Committee of Users and Operators of the Port of Genoa, the town, province and district councils, and with public administrative bodies such as the Harbor Office and the Customs Office.

The aim of the port is to develop the traffic line between Europe and Asia. Potential growth areas are in container, passenger, and cruise traffic, and in ship repair. The port is unable to expand along the coast because the town surrounds the existing limits of the port. There exist three possibilities to accommodate any needed expansion. The first is to rationalize the port's use of land to make it more efficient. The second is to recover the area abandoned by manufacturing industries for new port uses. The third possibility is to expand the port seaward through reclamation. It was within these scenarios that the Port Authority Plan Agency procured ideas from Koolhaas, Solà Morales and Smets. The utilization of design concepts imagines the port as a series of complex places and integrates this territory into a complete idea of the city.

The essential components of the New Port Master Plan are the reduction of iron and steel activities in the port, the rationalization of the oil port, the exclusion from the port territory of any new functions that are not compatible with environmental requirements, the creation of three new district parks, and the redevelopment of existing structures over the need for expansion. Many of these considerations deal with how to work with obsolete transportation infrastructure. This debate has included considerations for the redesign of the vehicular links for the port and the city with the goal of generating a functional independence between the two traffic flows. The San Benigo area is a good example of inefficiencies induced by thirty years of poor coordination between the port and the city, the result being the incremental addition of elements in response to particular demands – access roads, links, and lane widenings. The area is in any measure inefficient. The Master Plan acknowledges, in a very intelligent way, that relationships between the port, as the place of goods handling and of production, and the city are governed by different, and sometimes contradictory, rhythms and spatial needs.

The Master Plan divides the city into six areas – Voltri-Prà, Pegli-Multedo-Sestri, Cornigliano-Airport, Sampierdarena, Porto Antico, and the last is the area of Naval Repairs – Fiera-Piazzale Kennedy. The design schemes mentioned earlier deal with specific areas. Manuel Solà Morales' scheme for the Naval Repair District deals with a linear space that borders the port and the city. The scheme aims at a sectional separation of uses. The project suggests making use of the highest difference between the city and the docks by having urban traffic operate at the higher level and allowing industrial traffic and functions to occupy the space below.

The OMA proposal for the waterfront between Porto Antico and the Lanterna was similarly developed. It creates a great balcony overhanging the docks, which might become a suspended park connecting city landmarks, the ancient port, the new ferry terminal and the Lanterna. The OMA proposal suggests a direct connection between the ancient city and the sea. At the Darsena, the scheme introduces wedges of program that cut across linear boundaries, and provide moments of attraction to the water's edge.

Marcel Smets' scheme for the Cornigliano-Airport area deals with infrastructure improvements and a goods processing center to replace an existing hot-working steel plant. The scheme refocuses the hierarchical relationship between the main axis of road flows, the intersection junctions with the Genoa Cornigliano Motorway, the new road system in the Polcevera Valley, and the new District Park.

The waterfront of Las Palmas

The area of Vegueta is the historic center of Las Palmas and the site of the earliest European settlement. It is located at the mouth of the Barranco de Guiniguada. Cobbled streets and two-story colonial architecture define the area. The cathedral, the Museum of Columbus, Casa de Colón, the Fine Arts Museum, the Museo Canario, the Sacred Heart Museum of the Diocesis and the Courts of Justice are located in this area. The Mercado de Vegueta, the municipal market, is the oldest of four markets in the city and is located at the mouth of the Barranco de Guiniguada. The historic trade and administration area, located around the Calle Mayor de Triana, houses the Teatro Pérez Galdós, the Island Cultural Center, the Central Library, and the Presidency of the Autonomous Government. This area is now a pedestrian zone.

Most of the public authorities are located in the area around the Multiple Service Building. The Autonomous Government departments are located here. A number of institutional and administrative bodies are located in the area of Juan XXIII, such as the headquarters of the presidency of the Autonomous Government of the Canary Archipelago, the Department of Economy and Commerce, the Island Water Council, and the Comisaría de Policia (Police Headquarters). In the area around Mesa y López, in particular in the area between the Naval Base and the Plaza de España, is the main shopping area. The area has two large department stores constructed in the 1970s. The Parque Santa Catalina is one of the major tourist and recreation areas in the city, with restaurants and gift stores. This area has also been converted to a pedestrian zone. The beach at Las Canteras is a hub of leisure and tourism in the city, being a sandy beach some three kilometers long. The beach has hotels, apartments,

7.9 View across Puerto de la Luz, Las Palmas.

7.10 View down the Avenida Marítima, Las Palmas.

restaurants and outdoor cafés and bars. At the western end of the beach, in El Rincón, is the Auditorium Alfredo Kraus Convention Center.

Along the waterfront are a number of transportation infrastructures that both define the current situation of the waterfront and condition any future possibilities. The Avenida Marítima is a six-lane road, built in the 1970s to link Las Palmas with the south of the island, which carries most of the traffic generated by port activity and runs along the front of the city to provide a continuous façade of buildings. The C-811 is a four-lane motorway, located adjacent to the Guiniguada and links the municipalities in the center of the island – Santa Brigida, San Mateo and Tejeda – to Las Palmas. It is the major entry into the city for people who live in Tafira. Other minor streets include Juan XXIII, one of the most important streets in the city, and Avenida José Mesa y López, which is one of the major shopping streets and links the Avenida Marítima with other parts of the city.

Various public bodies control the waterfront in Las Palmas. These bodies have responsibility for different aspects of the spatial organization along

7.11 Las Palmas waterfront.

the waterfront. In response to the disjointed nature of this situation, the Port Authorities of Las Palmas decided to combine resources to rethink the nature of a three-mile stretch of waterfront between Barranco Guiniguada and Santa Catalina. The aim of this exercise was similar to the Genoa effort in that it sought to unite the city with the waterfront whilst integrating port uses compatible with other urban functions.

With this goal in mind, the various public agencies have been working together to find an appropriate way to coordinate their respective efforts. Some efforts already taken, typically by isolated agencies, lack a coordinated effort. Studies have been undertaken by the Port Authorities of Las Palmas on the possible reuse of the Santa Catalina mole, the former Trasmediterránea building, the Sovhispan building and the Sanupú and Wilson moles. The Town Council of Las Palmas de Gran Canaria has undertaken studies on the rehabilitation of the Parque Santa Catalina and the surrounding area and has produced a municipal Master Plan for Las Palmas. The Puerto de la Luz de Las Palmas has undertaken studies for a variety of its properties. The Canary Government Department of Tourism and Transport has a project looking at an intermodal hub in Santa Catalina. The General Coastal Department of the Ministry of Environment has a plan for the remodeling of the Avenida Marítima Roadway. Finally, the Canary Government Department for Territorial Organization, together with the Town Council, has produced "The Special Waterfront Plan for the East Coast of Las Palmas de Gran Canaria." As one might expect, the waterfront in Las Palmas is a heavily contested zone. While these plans all aim at improving various aspects of the waterfront, a communal vision remains illusive.

The "Special Waterfront Plan" aims at establishing the systematic organization of the operations for the coastal margin along the east coast between the very north of Playa de Las Alcaravaneras and the extreme south of the beach at La Laja. The plan establishes and defines relationships from the seafront and the building façades on the west side of the Marine Parade, Avenida Marítima. This is a controversial document. The

7.12 Playa de San Augustin, Las Palmas.

scope of this area includes a stretch between Playa de Las Alcaravaneras and the cathedral, which is the service area of the port. This area is well connected to the city and somewhat removed from the port proper; however, it is still significant in terms of port operations.

In response to the "Special Waterfront Plan," the Puertos de Las Palmas produced their own document which outlines their perspective on operations along the waterfront between Guiniguada and Santa Catalina. This perspective sets out to present "the main limitations, conditioning factors and restrictions of a physical, legal, economic and planning nature for present and future operations on this stretch of waterfront" (Puertos de Las Palmas, 1997: 6).

The waterfront along this part of Las Palmas is reclaimed land protected by a breakwater. One of the major constraints on development is the height of the sea wall in relation to the water level, especially the low tide level. This height difference allows the outlets to be higher than the level of the sea. The height of the sea wall significantly limits possibilities for visual connections to the water's edge. The other barrier between the town and the water is the Avenida Marítima, which separates the breakwater, and the adjacent path from the city. The motorway has a very negative impact on the façade of the historic Vagueta. Any redevelopment of this stretch of the city must look at the relationship of the road to the water's edge and the façade of the city. Currently there are areas of active interest along this part of the city. These include the marina extension, the redevelopment of the Navy base into a shopping complex, and the bus station, which is under construction. Recently completed projects include the jet-foil terminal.

Conclusion

The stories of Genoa and Las Palmas serve to outline the nature of the waterfront as a contested territory. In Genoa, decades of dispute fundamentally eroded the quality of the waterfront as a place in the city.

7.13 View toward Puerto de la Luz, Las Palmas.

7.14 View toward Guanarteme, Las Palmas.

In Las Palmas, the continued fragmentation of decision-making in this zone means that the potential of the waterfront suffers. Other cities now aim to emulate the Genoa situation. In Genoa, the appreciation of the waterfront as a common territory, rather than a contested one, has changed the nature of decision-making between the Municipality and the Port Authority.

For planners and architects, the Genoa case is of particular interest for the role of "design thinking" in framing the discourse of development along the waterfront. The Port Authority Plan Agency's employment of ideas from Koolhaas, Solà Morales and Smets, allows for the engagement of design thinking in the formation of policy decisions. Too often designers arrive in a process after major decisions are set. The Genoa example displays the potential for design to be informative as well as reactive. Design thinking used in this way can both open the possibilities and define the specifics. It can operate at a global as well as a local level. It can influence the process and reclaim a role in the generation of urban environments. The utilization of design concepts imagines the port as a series of complex places and integrates this territory into a complete idea of the city. The application of design thinking can act as a unifier of common beliefs and identities.

The Genoa case is, unfortunately, the exception rather than the rule. Las Palmas is more typical in this sense. In Las Palmas, the City and the Port

7.15 Edge between city and port, Genoa.

7.16 View above Cristoforo Colombo Airport, Genoa.

Authority have different views for the same territory. However, there is an increasing dialogue between the two. Perhaps there is even a realization that it will take both groups to define the future of the waterfront in Las Palmas.

"Modern Ports and Historic Cities" was based in part upon case material prepared by the Port Authority of Genoa; by the Municipality of Genoa; and by Joaquin Casariego and Elsa Guerra of Las Palmas; and on presentations by Professor Bruno Gabrielli, Alderman for Urban Planning, the Historic Center and Urban Styling for the City of Genoa; Giuliano Gallanti, President of the Port Authority of Genoa; Vice Mayor and Town Planning Councillor for Las Palmas, Juan José Cardona González; and José Setién Tames, the Director of the Municipal Planning Office for the Municipality of Las Palmas at the Waterfronts in Post Industrial Cities Conference, October 7–9, 1999, Harvard Design School, Cambridge, Massachusetts.

References

Autorità Portuale di Genova (1999) *Piano, Porto, Città*, L'esperienza do Genova.

Hoyle, B. S. and D. A. Pinder (eds) (1981) *Cityport Industrialization and Regional Development*, Oxford.

Port Authority of Genoa (1999) *Quaderni Portuali – ports, transport and trade*.

Puertos de Las Palmas (1997) Reference Document for Remodelling of the Waterfront of Las Palmas de Gran Canaria, Stretch: Guiniguada–Santa Catalina, November.

http://www.palmasport.es/ingles/index.htm

http://www.portel.es/puertos.htm

http://www.porto.ge.it

http://www.progranca.com/en/index.html

http://www.provincia.genova.it/

8 Port and city relations
San Francisco and Boston

Anne Cook, Richard Marshall, Alden Raine

What do football stadiums, baseball stadiums, convention centers, and mixed-use commercial projects have to do with the relationship between ports and cities? On the waterfronts of many American cities these have quite a bit to do with each other. This comes from the changing nature of the waterfront, changes in the role of port authorities, and the redevelopment attitudes of many American cities. This chapter deals with the changing nature of the relationship between the port and the city in the American context by exploring two port cities: Boston and San Francisco.

Our intention here is to describe the complex relationships that occur between the port, the city, the state, and the public. Of interest to us is the resultant physical condition that manifests itself on the waterfront in these cities. Both of these locations have had to deal with obsolete infrastructure, competition and the increasing mistrust and criticism of the city's citizenry. In comparison, the waterfront contexts of San Francisco and Boston offer two quite distinct institutional structures. By exposing the characteristics of these, we hope to understand their influence on city building on the waterfront.

The American experience of city building is fundamentally different from the European and because of this there exists a fundamental difference between port and city relationships. In Europe, the factor of time forged a much stronger bond between ports and cities. Interwoven physically, politically and economically for centuries, this relationship has had a much greater influence on the urban morphology of European cities than in the United States. In America, cities were, for the most part, opportunistic and speculative in their spatial generation. They formed instantaneously to exploit resources or take advantage of trade routes; deployed the grid as an ideal tool for organizing the landscape quickly. The influence of the port had less impact on the spatial organization and physical layout of the modern American city than in Europe.

Besides history, there exist some fundamental differences between European and American waterfront development. There is, of course, some risk of generalization in talking about the contexts of Europe and America. Both are actually complex, culturally and politically fragmented places. One of the major differences, however, is that in Europe waterfront development informs national urban policy decision-making, the best-known example being that of the Netherlands. The British planning system, likewise, is unitary in that national waterfront legislation applies to the whole country and is mandatory (Cullingworth, 1994). Over the last couple of decades, there has been an increasing development of regional spatial planning in Europe. Although focused on transportation infrastructures, promoting such things as transport corridors and rail links, such spatial planning at a super regional scale obviously influences the development of port policy.

In the United States, a national urban policy does not exist. The last regional planning initiative, at the scale promoted in Europe, was the Federal Highway Act of 1949. Almost in direct opposition to the growth of regionalism in Europe, planning responsibility moved toward local control in the United States. Another difference, this time of degree, is the nature of participatory planning in the United States. In Europe national urban policy, and differences in the development role of municipalities, means that issues of community participation are inevitably different than in the United States. The era of the city as a large-scale developer ended with a series of large-scale disasters in the United States. Today, municipalities often lack both the financial resources and the confidence to tackle the scale of developments on the scale proposed on the Ij-banks in Amsterdam.

Boston and San Francisco provide two different types of port and city contexts. In Boston, planning and economic development come under the control of the Boston Redevelopment Authority (BRA). The port authority, Massport, is an independent public agency entrusted with developing, promoting and managing airports, the seaport and transportation infrastructure. Both Massport and the BRA fall under the control of the state for any development activity on the waterfront – in particular the auspices of the Secretary of Environmental Affairs. In San Francisco, by comparison, the port is structured the same way as any other city department, its commission is appointed by the mayor. The San Francisco Port Authority does enjoy some autonomy from the city, in that it is financially independent and revenues generated by the port can only be used for trust purposes. It is in the unique position that it must further statewide interests and do so without monies from the city's general fund.

Boston and San Francisco have rich waterfront histories. Boston was a major American trading port well into the nineteenth century, first between the colonies and Europe, and later for trade with the Pacific Northwest and China. Competition, obsolete infrastructure and the development of alternatives to sea transport eroded the place of the Boston waterfront after the First World War. The decline of the waterfront environment in Boston continued until the 1960s, when the city started to take active steps to create waterfront amenities. The urban renewal period in Boston was an attempt to revitalize a dying and deserted city as more people moved outward into the suburbs. The federal urban renewal program, established by the Housing Act of 1949, represented an unprecedented restructuring of the North American city. Boston was no exception. Major restructuring of districts in areas near the waterfront and in the downtown of Boston cost nearly $50 million. Since the early 1970s, significant efforts have helped to secure the waterfront as an urban amenity in the city.

San Francisco's relationship with its water edge dates back to the California Gold Rush, a time of tremendous expansion for the San Francisco Bay. This growth led to the creation of a State Commission in 1863 to improve the harbor. During the twentieth century, the waterfront became industrial finger piers, railroad terminals, warehouses and a logistics center for the Pacific theater during the Second World War. In the 1950s, San Francisco continued to be the premier cargo port for the West Coast. In 1968, the state transferred responsibility for the waterfront to the City and County of San Francisco. This, in turn, led to the establishment of the Port Commission. Today, shipping and ship repair are located primarily south of China Basin, while cruise ships, ferries, recreational boating and commercial maritime operations remain on the northern waterfront.

Reflections on the San Francisco waterfront

San Franciscans are blessed with a magnificent waterfront, characterized by the turgid waters of the Pacific along its west coast, and the tamer waters of San Francisco Bay on its north and east coasts. San Francisco's well-known hills drop steeply to the bay and, due to the city street grid so carefully laid upon them, San Franciscans and visitors alike enjoy spectacular views of the waterfront from almost any neighborhood of the city. Blessed with such breathtaking geography, the city's indefatigable residents have long advocated that protection and public enjoyment of the waterfront and its historic maritime character should be the guiding principle behind waterfront development.

Yet, for decades, San Francisco's northeastern waterfront has been largely inaccessible to the public. As its once thriving break-bulk piers became functionally obsolete, the San Francisco waterfront, like so many US ports, failed to make the transition to modern-day uses. Pier after pier fell into disrepair, making both public and private access impossible. Attempts to redevelop the waterfront by the San Francisco Port Commission, the city agency charged with managing the tidelands in public trust for the people of the state, were so out of step with the goals of the city's citizenry that project after project failed, and the Port Commission became the subject of increasing mistrust and criticism.

Over the past decade, however, a series of physical, regulatory and financial constraints on waterfront redevelopment, some unique to San Francisco and others experienced on post-industrial waterfronts throughout the United States and abroad, have been eased. In fact, it is the confluence of these changes which has permitted the transformation of the San Francisco waterfront from an underutilized resource to an area teeming with pedestrians and redevelopment activity. How this happened in a city where "NO" had become the almost universal response to the port's waterfront redevelopment proposals provides lessons which may be useful for redevelopment efforts in other post-industrial cities.

The port of San Francisco in transition

From 1863 until 1968, the port of San Francisco was controlled by a State Board of Harbor Commissioners, exempt from local control and backed by the vast financial resources of the state. The State Board guided the port from its infancy to the height of its maritime industrial activity during the Second World War. Post-Second World War, the rise of foreign competition in shipbuilding and repair dealt a severe blow to the port. In addition, the shift from break-bulk to containerized shipping reduced demand for San Francisco's cargo facilities. Today, despite significant investments to modernize its facilities, the port of San Francisco remains a niche port for cargo. San Francisco's remaining cargo operations take place at only a few piers in the far southern quadrant of the city, leaving the northeastern port lands ripe for redevelopment.

From the outset, the port's efforts to reuse its northeastern lands have been fraught with controversy. The State Board's early plans for redevelopment of the northeastern waterfront were clearly out of step with local views on appropriate waterfront uses. First, the State Board rejected surface level transportation improvements to the waterfront's Embarcadero Roadway because of concern that non-port traffic would interfere with the reuse of the port's finger piers. Instead, like so many waterfronts across the nation, in 1957 an elevated freeway was erected along San Francisco Bay, effectively removing the downtown waterfront from public view and use. Second, a plan generated by the state's World Trade Center Authority and endorsed by the governor called for construction of 7- and 30-story buildings to replace the historic Ferry Building. Third, in 1959, the State Board's "Embarcadero City" plan envisioned filling in the bay north of the Ferry Building to accommodate high-rise structures for non-maritime uses. The efforts of outraged citizens led to a groundswell of citizen opposition to the elevated freeway. Construction of the downtown portion of the freeway occurred before this citizen opposition ended the construction mid-span and the waterfront high-rise projects never got off the ground.

After these failures, responsibility for port lands transferred from the state to the city in 1968. As a condition of the transfer, the state required the city to create the Port Commission. The Commission holds complete authority to take all actions necessary to fulfill its public trust responsibilities to promote maritime commerce, navigation and fisheries, as well as to protect natural resources and develop recreational facilities for public use on port lands. To ensure that port assets would not be raided by the city, the transfer agreement required that the port remain financially independent of the city and revenues generated by the port only be used for trust purposes. Thus, although the port is structured much like other city departments (for example, its Commission is appointed by the mayor), it is unique in that it must further statewide interests and do so without monies from the city's general fund. Moreover, its duties are extremely varied.

Unlike some ports, which primarily manage shipping and/or airport operations, the port of San Francisco oversees a broad range of commercial, maritime and public activities. In some areas, like Fisherman's Wharf, maritime activities (in this case commercial fishing) have become the background amenity for the city's thriving tourist economy. In other areas, the port uses piers for maritime support services such as ship repair, tug and tow operations, and a Foreign Trade Zone, largely outside the public's consciousness. At the Ferry Building, commuter and recreational ferries bring commuters to San Francisco from other Bay Area cities. The remaining cargo operations still take place in the Southern Waterfront. The Port Commission oversees this myriad of activities, balancing the often-competing interests of maritime and commercial tenants, public trust responsibilities to the people of the state, and responsibilities to the people of San Francisco, whose waterfront it oversees. As history attests, this balancing act, which has never been an easy one, continued to confound the port and stymie revitalization during the first two decades of local control.

When the city gained control of the port in 1968, it assumed responsibility for outstanding state obligation bonds and agreed to invest an additional $100 million for harbor improvements. The city expected to generate the revenues for these investments through extensive new commercial development. To this end, the port proposed development of a 50-story US Steel Office Building located on fill between the Ferry Building and the Bay Bridge. In response to public outrage to this plan, the city's Planning Commission imposed a forty-foot height limit on most port property north of the Ferry Building. At the same time, the State Attorney-General's Office issued an opinion stating that the newly formed Bay Conservation and Development Commission (BCDC) could not permit non-water-oriented uses (e.g. offices and residential) on new bay fill. Consequently, the port's plans for the US Steel Building, and even more-ambitious projects to the north, never left the drawing board.

This pattern of misguided development expectations, quashed by regulatory revelations and public outcry, has repeated several times in the history of the port. In the process, housing, general office and private health clubs, among other uses, have generally been deemed unacceptable on the port's public trust lands. Most recently, a proposal for a sailing center with a hotel on piers 24 and 26 was defeated when San Francisco voters passed Proposition H in 1989.

Proposition H: the waterfront planning initiative

Displeased with the port's continuing attempts to develop ill-conceived, mega projects along the waterfront, San Francisco voters passed Proposition H in 1989, which placed a moratorium on non-maritime development along the shore until a waterfront master plan was developed. Proposition H included provisions aimed at addressing how the waterfront plan would develop if the port chose not to prepare it. Rather than delegate this task to the San Francisco Planning Department or Redevelopment Agency, the Port Commission elected to develop its own waterfront plan. It chose to do so, both because the unique nature and responsibility of the port were not readily understood by other planners, and to ensure that the plan was fully embraced by those who would be tasked with its implementation. The monumental challenge facing the port was to fulfill not just the letter but the spirit of Proposition H, by developing a waterfront plan that addressed maritime needs and community desires for greater waterfront accessibility. In addition, the aim of the plan was to rebuild public faith in the port.

As is the case in Boston, reaching consensus in San Francisco on any subject related to waterfront redevelopment is challenging. When it comes to consensus-based planning, what clearly is one of the city's greatest assets – its diverse, stimulating, well-educated and opinionated citizenry – is also one of its greatest challenges. This is especially true on the San Francisco waterfront where many were skeptical of the ability of the port to conduct an open and thoughtful planning process. To the surprise of watchdog groups, the port addressed these concerns head-on by taking the unprecedented step of creating a community-based waterfront planning process. The port first solicited applications for a 27-member Advisory Board with representatives from all walks of city and waterfront life. Members included representatives from the mayor's office, other elected officials and decision-makers, maritime, business, environmental, open space and urban design interests, and each neighborhood or district adjacent to port lands. The Advisory Board had the daunting task of independently recommending a waterfront plan for Port Commission consideration.

Port staff proposed, and the Advisory Board followed, a phased planning process which first focused on the port's complex regulatory environment and public trust responsibilities and included candid discussions of the port's history of failed projects. Next, with the help of expert panels, the Advisory Board thoroughly evaluated and reserved ample lands to meet the long-term needs of each of the maritime industries of the port. Only then did the Advisory Board broach the controversial topic of the extent to which non-water-dependent activities, such as commercial development, could be included in the plan to help activate the waterfront and subsidize maritime industries, public access and open spaces. The results of this unprecedented six-year public planning effort was a very flexible and award-winning Waterfront Plan which defines the acceptable uses, character, urban form and public amenities for the port-controlled waterfront, and which enjoys extremely widespread support.

Boston waterfront

The Boston Harbor is also a contested space. It includes a wide geography that has been dramatically altered over time. Indeed, the footprint of Boston today bears little resemblance to the original site of settlement. Today, the land added contains the wharf districts of the historic port, choice residential neighborhoods, the downtown waterfront, the modern seaport, Logan International Airport, and several of Boston's signature institutional and civic facilities. Ironically, today's waterfront policy debate reflects a deep-seated public resistance to further land filling and a passion for stewardship of those tidelands filled long ago.

As Bostonians demanded more space, tidelands filled. In addition to filling it, Bostonians have spent nearly four centuries doing one other thing to their harbor – making the water dirty and then cleaning it up. By 1980, Boston Harbor was desperately polluted and the target of parallel federal and state environmental lawsuits. In 1984, the governor and legislature created the Massachusetts Water Resources Authority (MWRA) and gave it the massive job of reinventing the region's wastewater conveyance, treatment, and discharge systems. In 2000, the job is almost complete.

By historical good fortune, however, the harbor has remained predominantly an area valuable for its natural beauty. Boston Harbor is blessed with an urban archipelago of thirty-seven islands, which over the centuries have accommodated year-round and summer communities, prisons, lighthouses, social institutions, rendering plants, treatment plants, trash dumps, fortifications, and public open space. Today, the islands are mostly clean, uninhabited, and open to the public. Now that the waters of the harbor are also clean enough to support recreation and tourism, thirty of the islands have been included in the Boston Harbor Islands National Recreation Area. Families that once scoffed at the polluted harbor now take ferries and water taxis to this unique ocean park.

For many Bostonians, in fact, the "rediscovery of the harbor" over the last fifteen years means the MWRA clean-up and the opening of the islands. However, two other stories have been unfolding as well – the modernization of Boston's seaport, and the debate about how best to recycle those portions of the urban waterfront left fallow by earlier changes in maritime business and technology.

Boston Harbor has always been a working seaport, and the evolution of maritime commerce – wax and wane, obsolescence and change – has been a constant. As recently as the Second World War, Boston was one of North America's great port cities, in activity level as well as public image. Long-term factors beyond the control of the maritime community have eroded that position: the opening of the St Lawrence Seaway; the downsizing of the navy; the out-migration of mass-production manufacturing; the erosion of the North Atlantic fishery; and the emergence of more centrally located "load centers" or "megaports" as linchpins of a restructured marine cargo industry.

Boston remains New England's only large, commercially diverse port, and the maritime sector remains a major economic contributor in absolute terms. The industrial port provides some 9,000 jobs and $2.8 billion annually in direct and indirect employment. Over 17 million tons of cargo moved through Boston in 1997, divided among containers, automobiles, dry bulk, and liquid bulk. One long-term factor that *has* helped the port is New England's increasing reliance on imported petroleum, which accounted for 12 million tons of the total. Boston's ocean cruise industry, all but dead fifteen years ago, is visible and thriving today. The seafood processing industry has stayed and modernized, even if much of the raw fish is imported rather than landed.

Massport

The institutional components of Boston Harbor are more complicated than in San Francisco. The key public actor in Boston's maritime industrial sector is the Massachusetts Port Authority, or "Massport." Created by the legislature in 1956 and operational since 1959, Massport is an independent revenue bond authority, whose seven-member board of directors is appointed by the governor to staggered, seven-year terms. Unlike the San Francisco Port Commission, Massport is a multimodal transportation agency which owns and operates not only the traditional seaport but also Logan International Airport and the Mystic Tobin Bridge, a principal harbor crossing. Massport formed by merging three formerly separate agencies: the Port of Boston Commission, the State Airport Board, and the Mystic River Bridge Authority. Only a handful of other American port authorities – among them New York / New Jersey, Seattle, and San Juan – have similar compositions.

From the outset, the assumption was that other facilities would cross-subsidize the port of Boston, which by the late 1950s was in obvious physical and economic decline. Thanks largely to the economic success of the airport, Massport has been able to sustain and grow all of its facilities without any state or local financial assistance. Overall, Massport employs 1,200 and supports 20,000 jobs on its premises. The airport, seaport, and toll road operations contribute more than US$5 billion annually to the regional economy.

In the last decade, Massport has invested over $100 million in the modernization and adaptation of the seaport. The key projects include doubling the capacity of Conley Terminal, the principal container facility; converting Moran Terminal, the older, more constrained container site, to a new, state-of-the-art automobile import center; building the new Black Falcon cruise terminal; and modernizing the Fish Pier. Massport also worked with federal officials to find an environmentally acceptable strategy for deepening the harbor channels. This is nearly complete.

It is important to understand, however, that the entire seaport does not fall within Massport's jurisdiction. At its creation, Massport inherited only those maritime properties owned by the Port of Boston Commission, and has acquired relatively little waterfront property since then. Consequently, the petroleum terminals in Chelsea Creek and the Mystic River – a critical regional resource – are purely private facilities (although Massport's sponsorship of the harbor-dredging program is essential to their viability). Equally important, Massport owns some but not all of the vast expanses of piers, wharves, and filled tidelands which housed the port activities of generations past. In East Boston, South Boston, and parts of Charlestown, Massport is the principal owner of fallow maritime land ripe for redevelopment. In the downtown, the North End, and the Charlestown Navy Yard – areas no less ripe for waterfront redevelopment – Massport does not own any land.

The water line in Boston: a maze of jurisdictions

Over the last fifteen years, the planning, regulation, and redevelopment of Boston's shoreline have become the subject of the most engaging and controversial land use debate in the city's recent history. Massport shares this mission with two other powerful public actors.

One is the Boston Redevelopment Authority (BRA); a powerful agency created and empowered by state legislation to serve as the city's urban renewal authority, industrial development corporation, and planning board. As a development agency, the BRA is an important landowner on the downtown, Charlestown and South Boston waterfronts. As the municipal planning agency, the BRA is responsible for waterfront zoning and local project reviews.

The other is the Commonwealth of Massachusetts. In the 1970s, Massachusetts became one of the first states to impose a comprehensive environmental impact review mechanism on all significant projects requiring state land, money, or permits. The Secretary of Environmental Affairs administers the Massachusetts Environmental Policy Act (MEPA). This rigorous program applies to all agencies created by state legislative action, including both Massport and the BRA. MEPA review, typically through a detailed Environmental Impact Report, is an essential feature of any proposed waterfront infrastructure or development project, and must be successfully completed before any state action can be taken.

For projects which involve development in the water, on piers, or in filled tidelands, the most important state action is the issuance of a tidelands license by the state's Department of Environmental Protection. A statute known as Chapter 91 of the Massachusetts General Laws governs these licenses, and to a great degree any discussion about waterfront development in Boston is a discussion about Chapter 91.

Chapter 91: Defining the water line in Boston

Chapter 91 is the statutory expression of the ancient legal doctrine that the tidelands (that is, the area below the historic high-water line) are held in trust by the public. This doctrine is found in the Justinian Code as well as in the British Common Law and followed the Crown to New England; the Colonial Ordinances of 1641–1647 contain the direct antecedents of today's law. In general terms, the public trust doctrine requires that the tidelands be used only for water-related activity or otherwise serve a proper public purpose, and that in any event the right to "fish, fowl, and navigate" are reserved to the public.

For over three centuries, the public trust law in Massachusetts was applied almost exclusively to the placing of piers or fill in "flowed" tidelands. In a landmark 1979 case, however, the state's Supreme Judicial Court found that even tidelands filled long ago remain subject to a requirement that they serve a proper public purpose and accommodate a continuing public right of use and enjoyment. Because of this ruling, the legislature amended Chapter 91 in 1983 and 1987, and the Executive Branch, under the leadership of Governor Michael Dukakis, set about writing a sweeping new set of Chapter 91 regulations.

While tidelands licensing is administered by the state's Department of Environmental Protection, the governor recognized that the recodification of Chapter 91 was about something much bigger than traditional permits. The new regulations would shape infrastructure, land use, and development issues along the entire Massachusetts coastline. In Boston Harbor, recodification meant a new set of rules for waterfront development just as the rediscovery of the harbor was gathering momentum. The drafting of new regulations became an inclusive, policy-driven process, anchored in the Cabinet rather than the bureaucracy. An advisory committee representing maritime, environmental, development and legal interests provided valuable input, and the rules were developed in close cooperation with both Massport and the BRA.

The Chapter 91 regulations rest on a few organizing principles:

- Viable maritime industrial sites, particularly those with deep-water berths, are preserved for maritime industrial use.
- Everywhere else, the watersheet and the immediate shoreline are reserved for water-dependent uses, including water transportation and public access.
- Developers must provide uninterrupted pedestrian access to the shore-line, supported by ample view corridors, convenient connections to adjoining streets, and a welcoming program of signage and site management.
- Buildings on piers over the water, and the ground floors of buildings on filled tidelands within 100 feet of the water, are reserved for "facilities of public accommodation" – retail, restaurant, hotel, civic, and other uses which welcome the public (unlike offices and residences, which do not).
- The massing and layout of mixed-use, non-water-dependent projects must allow maximum public use and enjoyment of the tidelands.

A particular goal of the new regulations was to promote greater harmony – both procedural and substantive – among the three main public actors. Massport, by the terms of its Enabling Act, has exclusive planning powers in the former "Port of Boston" area and makes a good claim for exemption from Chapter 91 licensing. On the other hand, Massport's emerging role as a redevelopment agency for vacant waterfront properties struck many as falling beyond the exclusivity intended by the legislature. The new regulations therefore clarified that Massport is exempt from Chapter 91 licensing for airport and maritime projects, but not for mixed-use development.

The BRA launched a comprehensive rezoning of the Boston waterfront in parallel with the state's recodification of Chapter 91, and it was soon clear that the two efforts shared similar goals and planning principles. The BRA named its new zoning concept "Harborpark," to emphasize the importance of public access and enjoyment. Mayor Raymond Flynn named senior state officials to the Harborpark Advisory Committee.

This collaborative approach enabled the state's Chapter 91 team to solve what was known as the "one size fits all" dilemma. The new regulations clearly needed to address issues like height, lot coverage, setback from the water, and use restrictions, but no single approach would work. The Massachusetts coastline is a diverse mix of natural areas, villages, and small cities – and, in a category by itself, Boston. The solution, negotiated with the BRA, was to set relatively narrow "default" standards in the Chapter 91 Regulations. At the same time, this empowered cities and towns to prepare Municipal Harbor Plans, allowing alternatives more suitable to the harbor in question to replace these Chapter 91 standards. Once the Secretary of Environmental Affairs approved a Municipal Harbor Plan, the locally drafted substitute provisions would become the operative Chapter 91 standards for state licensing purposes. The BRA immediately prepared, and the state approved, Municipal Harbor Plans for Boston's Downtown, North End, and Charlestown waterfronts.

At the same time, the state, Massport, and the BRA agreed on a "belt and suspenders" approach to prevent the loss of viable maritime sites. A decade earlier, the state had defined a series of Designated Port Areas ("DPAs") in several harbors. In Boston, the DPAs included sites owned by Massport, the BRA, and private parties. Originally, these designations aimed to guide public planning and investment decisions. The new Chapter 91 Regulations went much farther, restricting DPAs to maritime industry and commerce and directly supportive ancillary uses. At the same time, the BRA created a parallel zoning category, the Maritime Economy Reserve ("MER"), and applied it to Boston's Designated Port Areas. In the mid-1990s, Massport and the BRA collaborated on the *Port of Boston Economic Development Plan,* an unprecedented blueprint for appropriate use of the DPA / MER properties.

A new era at the port of San Francisco

The institutional situation in San Francisco, despite appearances, is no less bureaucratic, even if the waterfront lies under the auspices of one agency in the Port Commission. However, since the waterfront plan's adoption in 1997, the waterfront re-use projects of the port are rapidly moving forward in an atmosphere of unprecedented support and excitement. In April 2000, when the first pitch was thrown at the San Francisco Giant's new waterfront ballpark, San Franciscans and visitors alike experienced firsthand the pleasure of recreating on the new San Francisco waterfront.

In December 2000, the port moved into new offices in the restored Pier One warehouse building which is being rehabilitated by a private developer and placed on the National Register of Historic Places. The move of the port will allow rehabilitation of the neighboring Ferry Building, the city's second most important civic building after City Hall, to begin. The Ferry Building's first floor will return to public use, providing a vibrant market hall and commercial recreation venue for ferry riders who pass through daily and for downtown office workers and visitors to the waterfront. Behind the Ferry Building, construction is well underway on the Downtown Ferry Terminal Project which will provide new berthing and passenger facilities for the ever-increasing ferry riders on San Francisco Bay. Developers have been selected for a new hotel project across from the shore near the foot of Telegraph Hill, for a $300 million cruise terminal and mixed-use project in the heart of the burgeoning South Beach neighborhood, and for two restaurants in the new Rincon Park at the foot of the Bay Bridge.

The port is in the process of offering three additional development opportunities: a new visitor-oriented attraction in the heart of Fisherman's Wharf, a new Chelsea Pier-type recreational development halfway between Fisherman's Wharf and the Ferry Building, and a historic preservation and mixed-use development project in the southern waterfront adjacent to the port's dry-dock operations.

Clearly, the economy has played a large role in stimulating developer interest in pursuing these waterfront projects. Yet, they would not be proceeding if the port had not restored citizen support for the port and its redevelopment efforts through the waterfront planning process. Each of the projects now under way is consistent with the plan, and has received the support of advisory groups formed specifically to help define and reach consensus on project goals and objectives prior to issuing requests for proposals to the development community. The projects have efficiently proceeded through, or appear destined to proceed through, the complex regulatory process of the waterfront. The San Francisco Planning Commission has amended the city's Master Plan to ensure consistency with the waterfront plan, and the Bay Conservation and Development Commission is in the process of following suit. In addition, these agencies have committed to join the port in providing early project design and to use review to eliminate the uncertainty so long faced by developers pursuing projects on the San Francisco waterfront.

Boston's waterfront

The Boston waterfront, as in San Francisco, is both a working port and the location for tremendous commercial real estate investment. The port of Boston competes with other major east-coast ports, including New York, which is less than a day's sail away. Because of this, it is undergoing revitalization for increased industrial, commercial, tourism and recreational uses.

Boston's maritime history has been written primarily in the four districts which frame the city's Inner Harbor: the Downtown/North End, Charlestown, East Boston, and South Boston. Created by filling tidelands, each of these waterfronts has undergone a cycle of maritime growth and obsolescence, resulting in vacant or fallow land ripe for reuse. While much of Boston's waterfront revival has yet to occur, some trends, some lessons, and some issues are already evident.

The Downtown/North End, Boston's original waterfront, was isolated from the rest of the city by construction of the elevated Central Artery in the 1960s. A primary purpose of Boston's massive "Big Dig" project is to place this expressway underground, reconnecting the waterfront to the downtown financial district and the historic North End neighborhood. Some of the wharves in this area retain their historic building stock, while others were cleared by the BRA and redeveloped with a mix of uses, including the New England Aquarium and an adjacent ferry and harbor cruise terminal.

Private development in the Downtown/North End area provides an evolution lesson in waterfront planning. The first such development was Harbor Towers, a high-rise luxury apartment complex built on a BRA wharf in the 1960s with no public access, closed lobbies, and a residents-only marina – a complete privatization of public tidelands. The Chapter 91 and Harborpark initiatives produced very different results. Rowes Wharf and the recently approved Battery Wharf include luxury residences also, but they are combined with hotels and restaurants, lively public uses on the ground floor, destination-quality outdoor spaces, year-round water transportation, and continuous, high-quality public use of the entire perimeter. The developer of Rowes Wharf was required to build and maintain one of the harbor's main ferry terminals as an integral part of the project.

East Boston, the home of Logan International Airport, has a long maritime history, including the yards where Donald McKay built America's greatest clipper ships. Today, obsolete wharves and piers, some of which have deteriorated to mere pile fields, dominate three sides of East Boston. The most attractive and intact segment of the East Boston waterfront is the one that faces across the Inner Harbor to downtown. Massport owned this segment, once a row of grain terminals and shipyards. In the 1990s Massport made an important decision to retain viable maritime operations – a ship repair yard and a tugboat terminal. However, in partnership with the city and community, it would redevelop the bulk of the piers and adjoining backlands. Today, part of the site has become one of Boston's most spectacular waterfront parks, and a private developer will build housing on the remainder.

The Charlestown Navy Yard has operated continuously since the late 1700s, and is still home to the USS *Constitution*, the world's oldest commissioned warship and flagship of the Atlantic Fleet. In 1974, the Navy closed virtually the entire yard. The BRA purchased it shortly thereafter and set about creating a redevelopment plan, reinventing the infrastructure, and recruiting developers. A blend of historic preservation and new construction, the reuse of the Navy Yard is one of the most extensive mixed-use urban renewal projects ever undertaken in the US. For the last decade, an approved Municipal Harbor Plan, in conformity with Chapter 91, has guided the process.

The total buildout potential for the Navy Yard is 4.3 million square feet. Today about half of the yard has been redeveloped, including the adaptive reuse of twenty historic buildings. Some 1.2 million square feet of office and medical research space and 1,250 housing units have been produced, along with marinas, restaurants, and another of the city's signature waterfront parks. Over the next twenty years, the BRA anticipates additional development in each of these categories, as well as a major hotel and civic facility.

The challenge of the South Boston waterfront

As important as each of these three districts is to the future of Boston Harbor, none is as complex, as challenging, as promising, or as controversial as the South Boston waterfront. Recognized two decades ago as Boston's urban development frontier, this 1,000-acre swath of filled tidelands borders the downtown financial district, the Inner Harbor, and the South Boston neighborhood.

Although the entire district was originally filled for maritime use, planners have long understood that the South Boston waterfront is really two worlds. Roughly speaking, the eastern half is and must remain the heart of Boston's long-term seaport economy. This area is home to Boston's principal container, mixed cargo support, ocean cruise, fish processing, and dry-dock facilities and has a critical mass of industrial infrastructure in place. The western half, which is within walking distance of the financial district and bustling South Station, is a mix of historic loft buildings along Fort Point Channel and long-vacant railyards along the Inner Harbor. This area represents a unique regional opportunity for mixed-use, transit-oriented development in a dramatic waterfront setting.

The city, state and Massport have spent fifteen years planning and building the infrastructure investments required to unlock this district. Thanks to the "Big Dig" project, the South Boston waterfront will soon enjoy direct underground expressway links to the interstate highway system and Logan International Airport. The surface roadway system is being completely restructured to create dedicated truck routes for the port area and an urban street grid for the mixed-use area. The Silver Line, an underground, high-capacity busway, will link the entire district to the downtown transit network and the airport. Thanks to Chapter 91, private developers will build and maintain water transit terminals capable of connecting significant volumes of people to the airport, the harbor, and the suburbs. Today, the South Boston waterfront contains some 14 million square feet of built space. Transportation planners believe that the infrastructure now planned and committed can accommodate an additional 17 million square feet – a generation's worth of new development.

In 1997, the city and state committed to one more public investment of transforming dimensions when they chose the South Boston waterfront as the site of Boston's new convention center. This $695 million facility, with 600,000 square feet of contiguous exhibit space, is being built on a 60-acre site in the westerly, mixed-use half of the larger waterfront district. The Convention Center is expected to stimulate the development of several hotels and to help animate the entire mixed-use area.

Massport plays a major, multifaceted role in the South Boston waterfront, primarily as the largest landowner in the eastern half of the district and steward of the core facilities of the working port. By investing directly in these properties, protecting them from incompatible development and advocating for truck route capacity to serve them, Massport not only promotes the port economy but also helps legitimize non-maritime, mixed-use development in the area closer to downtown.

Massport is also the largest landowner in the mixed-use area, with approximately 60 acres in the section known as Commonwealth Flats. These holdings include Boston's World Trade Center (the redeveloped Commonwealth Pier), the Boston Fish Pier, and extensive backlands. It is here that private developers under lease from Massport have built the Seaport Hotel and the first of several planned office buildings. These Massport development initiatives are meant to blaze the trail for other private investment in the area, while raising revenue to defray the seaport budget. They have been well received by the public and the BRA.

Most of the time Massport and the BRA share a good working relationship. Massport stumbled only once in this regard, albeit dramatically, when in 1997 it attempted to locate a new football stadium for the New England Patriots on 60 acres of land east of D Street, in the working port half of the waterfront district. The South Boston residential neighborhood vehemently opposed this project for fear of the traffic and noise impacts, while the maritime community opposed the reallocation of a large piece of land assumed to be in maritime reserve to a permanent non-maritime use.

Mayor Thomas Menino sided with the stadium opponents, and the BRA made it clear that if Massport persisted, it would litigate the question of whether Massport's statutory exemption from local zoning applied to non-maritime, non-airport projects. Massport backed away from the stadium proposal, and agreed to negotiate an agreement with the BRA whereby its non-maritime development projects on the South Boston waterfront would be reviewed as if subject to zoning. The episode is illustrative for two reasons: it involved a rare dispute over the limits of Massport's autonomy, as well as a perceived challenge to the long-term balance of land uses in South Boston.

The BRA's role in the South Boston waterfront is also multifaceted, beginning with land ownership. As owner and steward of the Boston Marine Industrial Park in the eastern half of the district, the BRA, like Massport, is a direct investor and advocate in the maritime economy. The BRA was also given the job of assembling the site for the Convention Center. However, the BRA's most important and controversial task in South Boston involves its role as the city's planning agency. With the major land use and infrastructure assumptions in place, the city turned to the BRA in the late 1990s to prepare an encompassing plan for the South Boston waterfront district, and the result, the *South Boston Public Realm Plan,* was well received. It was when the BRA turned to the next logical step, the preparation of the Municipal Harbor Plan to harmonize local planning with Chapter 91, that widespread controversy arose over the details of mixed-use development along the Inner Harbor and Fort Point Channel faces of the district. Constituencies differed over the appropriate scale of development, the proper balance of housing, offices, and other landside uses, and competing visions of how best to create open space along the water's edge. This is no idle exercise; an approved Municipal Harbor Plan is essential for development of the scale and complexity envisioned.

Conclusion

The new excitement and interest in waterfront redevelopment has also been spurred by monumental changes in the physical character of the waterfront. In San Francisco, after citizens mounted several unsuccessful efforts aimed at removing the Embarcadero Freeway, nature intervened in the form of the Loma Prieta earthquake in 1989. The earthquake wreaked havoc on many waterfront resources, from homes in the Marina District to the Bay Bridge and its connector freeways. As is often the case with tragedies, there was also a positive aspect for the port of San Francisco. Federal funds became available to repair damaged piers, which the port would not otherwise have been able to modernize. Because the earthquake rendered the freeway unsafe, the Embarcadero Freeway came down. The city has since spent over $500 million to transform the waterfront's Embarcadero Roadway. The Roadway transformed from an industrial road designed to accommodate freight trains and serve cargo piers, to a world-class waterfront boulevard resplendent with public art, historic signage, new historic trolleys from around the world, and a three-mile-long promenade along the shore. The city is now placing the final touches on the crown jewel of the new Embarcadero Roadway, a magnificent public plaza where the elevated freeway once stood in front of the historic Ferry Building. The removal of this physical and psychological barrier to the water's edge has been a major factor in the port's successful efforts to reunite the city with its waterfront.

Boston has not suffered any major earthquakes. However, in a historical sense the changes in the physical form of the waterfront have been no less dramatic. Hills were raised and shorelines molded to the make the profile of the Boston waterfront as we know it. Given some of what is happening on the Boston waterfront now, it appears that earthquakes may actually occur in Boston – but only in boardrooms and community halls! However, the current tension over the South Boston Seaport District Plan is rare when one views the history of waterfront development in Boston. In addition, this tension exists, to the degree that it does, between the state and the city, rather than between Massport and the city.

With a decade's worth of public planning and investment in place, and with Boston's booming real estate market having focused at last on the South Boston waterfront, there remains a question in the year 2000 as to whether a critical mass of high-quality, mixed-use development will be realized on the South Boston waterfront anytime soon. The underlying reason, as in most American cities, is that land use is debated publicly, decisions are legally and politically susceptible to intense public participation, and different people want different things.

Ironically, the issue which dominates the waterfront planning debate in so many port cities – the spatial competition between the maritime and urban development sectors for land and water resources – was largely solved in Boston a decade ago. The Chapter 91 Regulations, and the broad public policy agreements among Massport, the BRA, and the state which made them possible, addressed the space allocation issues in general. The broadly understood division of the South Boston waterfront into two halves, one maritime and one mixed-use, addressed those issues in the largest and most complicated of the waterfront settings. What remains to be seen is whether the current lack of consensus on a seemingly narrower issue – the ideal nature of mixed-use development – will be a momentary or enduring obstacle to progress.

The San Francisco experience in waterfront redevelopment is an interesting comparison to Boston. The San Francisco waterfront is controlled by one agency, one vision and one layer of bureaucratic control. Despite this, the people of San Francisco reprimanded the Port Commission by voting for Proposition H. Perhaps most interesting to note about San Francisco's experience is that Proposition H, which at the time seemed disastrous to the port, has, in retrospect, been a blessing. Proposition H focused the port's energies on comprehensive planning and community outreach during the early 1990s, when developers were retrenching. When the economy improved the port was ready to respond with a publicly embraced blueprint for reconnecting the city and the waterfront.

In Boston, achieving a world-class waterfront means negotiating the institutional relationships between several major players. For the greater part of Massport's history, an atmosphere of mutual trust and cooperation has prevailed between the port and the city. This is critical to Boston's efforts. One of the problems of dealing with two independent agencies, as we have seen in Las Palmas and other places, is that the unique nature and responsibility of the port is not readily understood by other planners. The issue compounds when the city does not fully control the waterfront, and the Port Authority does not have a mission to make the "city" waterfront but has a mission to finance airport and seaport projects. It naturally must do everything it can to maintain its bond rating. The authority's public trust responsibilities are therefore different from those of the city. Boston's success comes from constant dialogue between Massport and the BRA. For Boston to achieve its waterfront aspirations, this dialogue must continue.

A truly world-class waterfront is one that has a vision, both for the working aspects of the port and for the urban character of the city edge. Because of the nature of the San Francisco institutional arrangements, the same agency can strive for both. Even if it needed a reminder of this through the pain of Proposition H, the San Francisco Port Commission has taken this on as its role. In the case of Boston, such a holistic vision must rely on cooperation between two public agencies. In both cities, the waterfront provides a tremendous opportunity to make a vision for the future. One hopes that we will all be able to enjoy the results.

References

Boston Redevelopment Authority (1999) *The Seaport Public Realm Plan*, City of Boston, February.

Cook, Anne, Kari Kilstrom and Diane Oshima (2000) *The Port of San Francisco Waterfront Land Use Plan* (Republished version), January.

Cullingworth, Barry (1994) "Alternative planning systems: is there anything to learn from abroad?," *Journal of the American Planning Association* 60 (2): 162–172.

Luberoff, D. (1996) *Mega-project: A Political History of Boston's Multi-billion Dollar Artery/Tunnel Project* (Rev. edn), Cambridge, Mass.: Taubman Center for State and Local Government, John F. Kennedy School of Government, Harvard University.

Malone, P. (ed.) (1996) *City, Capital and Water*, London and New York: Routledge.

Perkins, G. (1986) *Boston's Waterfront: A Storied Past and a Brightening Future*, BRA Research Department Publications, Report no. 268, Boston, Mass.: Boston Redevelopment Authority Research Dept.

Vennochi, J. (1998) "Profit center: harbor development presents a huge economic opportunity for the region – if we can catch the wave," Special Section, *Boston Globe*, October 25, Sunday City Edition, p. 21.

www.Massport.com

PART V
NEW WATERFRONTS IN HISTORIC CITIES

9 Waterfronts, development and World Heritage cities
Amsterdam and Havana

Richard Marshall

The relationship between historic cities and new development is of critical interest for older cities contemplating development of their water's edge. The opening up of large tracts of land in these zones creates tremendous opportunities to re-engage historic city centers with their adjacent water areas. Waterfront redevelopment allows for new civic expressions that can reinforce the character and quality of the historic core. In doing so several considerations need to be addressed. What is the appropriate form of this development? How does one protect the historic city from the consumptive nature of newer development? How can meaningful relationships be established between the old and the new? How does new, often large, development situate itself amongst older, smaller fabric?

It is widely held that if a city does not grow and change it will stagnate. A city's health is equated to its growth. Just as strong is the belief that the preservation of our built historic fabric is important to the creation of identity and the preservation of character. These two positions are obviously at

9.1 Model of Havana.

odds with each other. These competing agendas often focus on the same territory in a city. Amsterdam and Havana provide two cases where this balancing act between development and preservation occurs. Both deal with the pressure of real estate exploitation for capital gain over the desire to save the physical residue of history. These conflicting ideologies are at the heart of waterfront development in these cities.

The comparison of Amsterdam and Havana shows insights into these considerations. Havana already is, and Amsterdam is to be, a UNESCO World Heritage City. Amsterdam has been dealing with the redevelopment of its waterfront for some thirty years. The story of the Amsterdam waterfront is one of success and failure, it has both positive and negative lessons to share. Amsterdam is a city founded on water. The city sits on top of a marshy peat bog and much of the older fabric of the city responds to a series of dikes constructed as early as the fourteenth century – forming the Damrak (Meyer, 1999). Despite the importance of water to its foundation, however, it turned its back on its waterfront in the late nineteenth century. The construction of Amsterdam's Central Station broke the relationship between Amsterdam and the River Ij. For most of the last thirty years, the re-establishment of this connection has been of central concern in waterfront redevelopment efforts. The relationship between the older fabric of the city and new developments, and making connections between them, is central to any discussion on the Amsterdam waterfront.

Havana, in comparison, is just now beginning to deal with similar issues. The waterfront in Havana is now a critical part of that city's redevelopment initiatives. The victory of the Revolution on January 1, 1959 marked a shift in priorities in Cuba from urban to rural development. Very little development occurred in Havana between 1960 and the middle of the 1990s. Because of this, the rampant commercial development that occurred in the 1960s and 1970s, common in other Caribbean cities, did not occur in Havana. Unfortunately, the priorities of the government and the economic situation in Cuba also meant that much of the basic upkeep of the city did not occur. The result is that Havana is both a precious historic artifact and a city in desperate need of maintenance, repair and modernization.

Amsterdam

Amsterdam is located about fifteen miles from the coast of the North Sea. It is the central city in the north part of "Randstad Holland," where more than one-third of the Netherland's population lives. The landscape of Amsterdam displays the impact of man over an extended period. Since the twelfth century lakes have been diked and marshes reclaimed. The swampy stratum of Amsterdam has always posed building problems. The topsoil consists of weak strata in the form of peat that is many feet thick, under which is a layer of clay and sand. Such conditions mean that structures were of light timber frames with wooden piles sunk into the ground to depths up to sixty feet.

Amsterdam's economy is multifaceted and includes trade, financial services, health care, education, industry, construction, and other businesses. Leading industries include, shipbuilding, sugar refining, publishing and the manufacture of heavy machinery, paper products and clothing. Amster-

dam Schipol Airport, the port of Amsterdam, and the telecommunications campus, known as Teleport, are the primary "ports" or entrances into the city. Amsterdam is the cultural and financial capital of the Netherlands. It is also one of the world's largest, conserved, historic inner cities. Amsterdam is a case study of innovative development and urban revitalization.

The historic city was established around a dam that separated the Amstel River from the Ij River (pronounced Ay), a former tributary of the South Sea. The River Ij was Amsterdam's connection to the world and until the decision to build the Central Railway Station (1882–1889) there was an open connection between the city and the sea. With the construction of the station, it was no longer the Ij Harbor but rather the Central Station that became the umbilical cord of the inner city. Although the harbor continued to play an important role for Amsterdam, the city essentially turned its back to it.

The inner city of Amsterdam has approximately 80,000 residents and supports 80,000 jobs. In the 1960s, the number of jobs was double this figure but, due to a lack of space and poor accessibility, the large financial corporations moved from the center to the periphery of the city. The old center, obviously not designed to accommodate motor vehicles, is well suited for pedestrians, bicyclists and public transportation. Unfortunately, there is a continuing pressure wrought by cars and tour buses in the inner city.

Amsterdam is a multi-polar city. International business and banking companies are located along the south axis of the city. Large-scale entertainment facilities are located around the new Ajax soccer stadium. Meanwhile, the inner city remains the most important center for culture, tourism and retail activities and for new forms of creative economic activity. These centers do not compete with one another; rather, they are complementary to each other's primary roles.

For most of its evolution, Amsterdam grew in a series of half-circles, starting at the core area along the Ij and gradually expanding away from it. Thus, the medieval city lies at the center of this semicircular plan, surrounded by the seventeenth-century canal belt, with its neat rows of trees and streets stretching out along the curvilinear waterways. The nineteenth- and early twentieth-century expansions also neatly fit around the historic core. In the middle of last century, however, Amsterdam instigated the General Expansion Plan. This plan authorized new growth areas, known as "lobes," which stick out like spokes from the older parts of the city. The General Expansion Plan of Amsterdam carried out by the Public Works Department from 1928–1934 is the first comprehensive example of CIAM functional town planning. Sigfried Giedion's *Space, Time and Architecture* and José Luis Sert's *Can Our Cities Survive?* both designate it such a place in history.

Havana

Havana, is a peculiar twentieth-century city due to its political and economic isolation. Since 1959, it has avoided much of the disastrous development that befell other cities around the world. At the same time, the provision of much-needed housing and infrastructure in the rural parts of the country has meant that the infrastructure of the city was not maintained. The city is now in desperate need of repair.

Cuba is an archipelago which includes some 4,000 islands. The city of Havana is on the main island's northwest coast, in a protected bay, the Bahia de Habana. Le Ciudad de la Habana (city of Havana) is one of Cuba's fourteen provinces and covers some 750 square kilometers, incorporating fifteen municipalities. Industrial production commands the prime position in Cuba's development plans. Much of the country's industry is focused on agricultural production, which includes food processing and packing factories, distilleries and flour mills. Other industrial sectors include

9.3 Map of Havana waterfront.

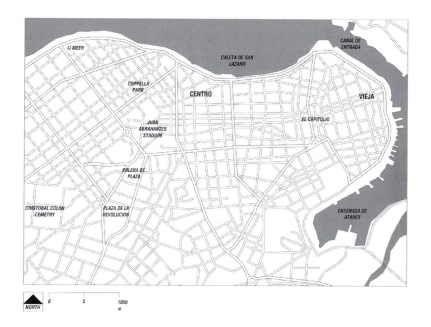

9.4 Ongoing restoration project, Havana.

sugar, petrochemical and oil refining, textiles, metals (including nickel, copper, chrome, silver, iron and manganese), chemicals, paper and wood products, cement, fertilizers, and consumer products.

Cuba is in an economic transition caused by the collapse of the former Soviet bloc. Figures from 1988 indicate that the Soviet Union accounted for 65 percent of Cuba's exports. In 1995, Havana announced that the GDP had declined by 35 percent in the period from 1989 to 1993. This is the result of lost Soviet support by means of soft loans and higher prices for Cuban products. In response to this, Havana has focused on attracting investment through real estate joint ventures. This has created a new market for housing directed to foreigners, and with the UNESCO designation of Havana as a World Heritage City in 1982, tourism has become a major growth industry in Cuba. Foreign investment and tourism bring with them both the hope of economic prosperity and the threat of harm to the architectural treasure that is Havana. The ability to balance the demands of capital with historic conservation is the major issue facing the city today.

Christopher Columbus discovered Cuba in 1492. Before Spanish occupation, it was the home to Carib and Arawak peoples. The town of San Cristóbal de la Habana, founded in 1514, was the westernmost city under the control of Diego Velázquez. The first settlers abandoned the original site of settlement after several unsuccessful attempts, and established the location of the present city in 1519 next to the port of Carenas. With the opening up of the New World, the deep-water, protected port in Havana became a strategic stop for traders. The Spanish colonization of South America saw tremendous wealth pass through Havana on its way back to

Spain. With the discovery of the trade winds to Asia, Havana became a major port for international trade for nearly two hundred years.

By the 1570s, Havana took measures for the defense of the city. French pirate Jacques de Sores attacked and burnt the Fuerza Castle when he seized Havana in 1555. Subsequently rebuilt in stone to a renaissance design, it is the oldest European fortification in the western hemisphere (1558–1577). In 1762, the English conquered Havana and held it for eleven months before Charles III of Spain traded Florida for the return of Havana. Once in the hands of the Spanish, Havana started the construction of more fortification including the Artarés, El Principe and the largest fortress in the Americas, San Carlos de La Cabaña.

By the turn of the eighteenth century, Havana was the third largest city in the New World, after Mexico and Lima. As the city's wealth increased, merchants began building magnificent three-story town houses, and the city started to expand. The Spanish governor, the Marques de la Torre constructed the Alameda de Paula, the first boulevard outside of the city walls. He also constructed great warehouses along the waterfront. In 1863, the city had grown to a point where boulevards were constructed west of the city beyond the walls of the old city.

Through the late nineteenth century tensions rose between the Peninsulares (native Spaniards) and the Criollo (Cuban born) inhabitants, including the wealthy white Criollo patrician families. These tensions ultimately led to the wars of independence but also led to competition in the construction of public edifices. This legacy includes the neo-classical El Templete (1828), the Teatro Tacón, and the remodeling of the Paseo de Carlos III, both completed between 1834 and 1838. In 1880, the Cuban hero, José

9.5 View across Havana.

Mantí founded the Cuban Revolutionary Party to start the first of three wars of independence. In 1898, in the midst of the war between Spain and Cuba, the USS *Maine* mysteriously sank in Havana Harbor. This event led to the establishment of a US military administration in Havana, which initiated several city-making constructions, including the famous Malecón along Havana's waterfront.

Cuba became an independent republic in 1902; however, the US continued to exert influence and the Cuban Revolutionary Party continued with its struggle against a series of corrupt puppet governments. By late 1958, Cuban forces led by Fidel Castro held most of the countryside and the US government withdrew its support for the Batista government. On January 1, 1959, the Revolution claimed victory.

Immediately before the Revolution, Havana was a highly developed city. The skyline displayed a series of skyscrapers, including the FOCSA building and the Havana Hilton. This was in contrast to the housing slums and tenements tightly set into the fabric of the city. One of the first initiatives of the Castro government was to initiate education and health care programs, and the construction of mass housing. With the top priority directed to the massive problems in the countryside, resources were not sufficient to stop the deterioration of the physical fabric of Havana. In a positive sense, the commercialization that occurred in many other South American cities did not occur in Havana.

Havana shares a common association with Amsterdam in relation to CIAM. In 1959, just before the victory of the Revolution, José Luis Sert completed work on a Master Plan for Havana. This plan imagined a major restructuring to the Malecón and to the heart of the old city. With the shift in priorities from the city to problems in the countryside this plan was never realized. In hindsight, it would have been a disaster for Havana: the Sert plan would have demolished major sections of the city that today are integral to the attraction of the city.

New waterfronts in Amsterdam

Discussions about the redevelopment of the land along the Ij began in the early 1980s. Before this period many cities experienced a decline in harbor-related industry. In Amsterdam this decline started with the completion of the North Sea Canal in 1875 and continued through the twentieth century. The emptying out of port-related uses provided an ideal opportunity for the city. The redevelopment of the banks of the River Ij is of primary importance in re-establishing the connection between the historic city and the harbor. The shift in harbor activities away from the inner city has provided opportunities to remake these connections.

Interestingly, waterfront redevelopment in Amsterdam occurs without a comprehensive plan. Rather, waterfront development is opportunistic and strategic. Areas that become vacant and free for development and do not require the construction of an entirely new urban infrastructure are used to advantage. This type of strategic intervention has had some positive results. For example, the city has been able to adjust decisions on developments in response to shifting market expectations. These developments have occurred in several parts of the waterfront.

9.6 The new Metropolis Museum, Amsterdam.

One of the first redevelopment projects was in North Amsterdam, on the north bank of the Ij. Although the project has met with some criticism since it was completed it represents a bold approach to waterfront development. Of particular interest is the acceptance of contemporary modern architecture in this project. In the United States, contextualism has become a paralyzing aspect to large-scale urban development. Invented historicism and the simulation of an imagined vernacular are the only acceptable possibilities. Unfortunately, the results are often safe to the point of being banal. In Amsterdam, there is a complete denial of this position and instead an acceptance that each age produces its own architectural statements. The city of Amsterdam is a composition of various periods, each expressing themselves.

The Eastern Dockland was home for many harbor-related companies. In the 1960s and 1970s these companies either moved to the western harbor or closed down. This opened the area for residential development. To date more than 7,000 housing units have been built along with some commercial and retail facilities. This project has gained international recognition and been awarded numerous prizes. The Western Dockland area, an area of wood warehouses of the former "Houthaven," is also being redeveloped for residential use with some 900 residential units.

The Ij-burg area (Ij-lake), located east of the Eastern Harbor, is a development full of conflict. Following years of argument between the municipal government and very well organized environmental groups, the people of Amsterdam voted for residential development in the Ij-lake. Once completed, this development will remake a historic and cultural bond with the water. Ij-burg is a project that will provide some 18,000 new residential units immediately adjacent to the old core of the city. It is to be an island city on the southwestern edge of Ijmeer (Ij lake), the stretch of water located to the east of Zeeburgereiland. The project occurs on seven islands – Steiger Island, Haven Island, Strand Island, Buiten Island and the three Riet islands.

The Memorandum of Conditions, "Design for Ij-burg," which appeared in May of 1996, was the first in a series of publications on this new community. This document forms the basis for all the plans for Ij-burg. On September 4, 1996, the Municipality of Amsterdam made a formal decision to bring Ij-burg into existence. "Design for Ij-burg" gives some idea of the shape that the new community will take. Studies of various housing locations in the Amsterdam region have shown that there are few sufficiently large sites for housing in the immediate environment. The alternatives (in Haarlemmermeer or to the south of Amstelveen) either are further away than Ij-burg or are less readily accessible by public transport. The construction of Ij-burg will take place within a time-scale of more than ten years. Haven Island and the Riet islands are the first to start. The projects will be undertaken by various consortia, comprising joint initiatives of housing associations, project developers and investors.

Housing is the major component of all development on the Ij-bank, and social housing equates to 40 percent of this. This housing, provided by the government, in many cases led the development of the area. Private residential development is encouraged because of the high quality of the social housing provided.

In a densely populated city such as Amsterdam, it is desirable to put limits on the use of land. A century ago, the city democratically decided on a land-lease system. The city leases land but remains the owner of the property. In this way, the increased value of the land benefits the entire community and, in addition, prevents speculation. This allows the city to construct affordable housing in very desirable locations on the waterfront. This active land policy is an important instrument in determining rents and sale prices of units and avoids the unilateral composition of neighborhoods that might otherwise occur in a "free market" system.

Of the entire waterfront in Amsterdam, the greatest challenge has been the central area of the southern banks of the Ij. This area, on both sides of the Central Station, is owned by multiple parties and is in need of new infrastructure. Adjacent to a dam and to the rail tracks, this area consists of five islands created a century ago. The railway was the primary user of the area with yards located along the Ostelijke Handelskade. To complicate matters, in the 1960s a new main distribution center was built on the Oosterdoks island.

In 1984, the city started the planning process for this area by holding a design competition. However, it was not until 1990 that the Amsterdam Waterfront Finance Company (AWF) attempted, for a second time, an

9.7 Typical fabric of central Amsterdam.

integrated plan for the area. The AWF took the lead in this process and produced both a business plan and a compelling scheme designed by Rem Koolhaas. Financing the infrastructure for the development was very high. To cover this cost would have meant that all proposed office development be located on the banks of the Ij. This did not happen, as the market had already discovered the south side of the city. In 1994, the public–private partnership collapsed. The project proved too intense, had too great a financial risk, and would take too long to implement. Political fragmentation, board arguments and the downward demand for financial office space finally finished the AWF. After a brief period of reflection, the city took the initiative and passed a strategic memorandum entitled "Anchors of the Ij" in 1995.

"Anchors of the Ij" aims at working within the existing island structure. Each of the schemes for each island will be based on its own potential in terms of location, use and land ownership. The phasing of the project starts at the outer edges and works toward the Central Station. The program is quite diverse and varied. Housing will account for approximately 40 percent (3,000 residential units) of the development and of this 30 percent will be social housing. The diversity of the inner city is a source of inspiration for the schemes. The city is investing in infrastructure and designing high-quality public spaces.

At strategic locations, the city is investing in public buildings and in public squares – the so called "anchors." In this way, the municipality is seeding the development – laying the path for private developers. Depending upon the situation, the city looks for appropriate ways to work with users and landowners. Private developers, granted the majority of the project, have already prepared plans for almost all of the islands. Each plan has a specific program and architectural construction. The Public Space Plan is reinforcing the relationship between the islands and the historic city. Corridors that connect the islands to the inner city, especially the railway underpasses, are of special concern. It is along these corridors that the anchors are located, zoned for public uses. These "anchors" include the Science Center, new Metropolis, built on top of the Ij-tunnel pier designed by the Italian architect Renzo Piano; the Passenger Terminal designed by H.O.K.; the Music Center, located at the head of the Oostelijke Handelskade, designed by the Danish office of Nielsen, Nielsen and Nielsen; Silodam, where monumental grain silos are being transformed into living-work spaces, designed by MDVRV.

9.8 Car parking is a major issue within Amsterdam.

Unique for the Amsterdam waterfront project is the concept of the Central Station complex as a commuter island. This area, accessible for all methods of transportation, will undergo a radical change. The plan calls for a new underground metro station, expansion of the railway, a bus station located on the Ij side of Central Station situated above an automobile tunnel. The plan also calls for redevelopment and expansion of the Central Station and the construction of new public spaces in the area. The Station complex will offer space for new shops and services both for commuters and tourists.

An urban design plan is being prepared for the adjacent Oosterdok island by the Eegaraat Architect Association. These plans include the expansion of the present Chinatown from the inner city, construction of the new main branch of the public library, the conservatory, a cinema complex, and possibly the new Amsterdam Stock Exchange. This island will become the center of arts and sciences in Amsterdam.

The plans for the Oostelijke Handelskade are now under construction. The project includes hotels, business parks, and offices, combined with renovated storage houses of residential and commercial uses. On the Westerdok Island, the railway yards are being leveled to create a residential area with space for smaller businesses and offices. At the tip of the island, a spectacular complex which includes offices, a hotel, residential units and a new yacht club will follow. All of these projects include flexible and durable building structures, developed to accommodate any future change of use and function.

The public support for this waterfront project has been relatively positive

9.9 One of Amsterdam's canals.

despite the enormous intervention in the area. Community organizations, the business community, and planning professionals have generally been supportive of the approach and the plans. There are a few exceptions in places, one example being the squatters who have resisted leaving. The city, to its credit, works with these people, which includes artists, to keep rents relatively low in order to maintain the "start-up" nature of the area.

The water uses, described in the Public Space Plan, are extensive. In the former inner docks, the space is used for houseboats, barges, historic ships, tour boats and water transportation. On the Ij, the nautical demands for the long-haul trade influence the design of the quays to accommodate sea and river cruise ships. The canal shipping trade is getting its clearance places, passage harbors have to be able to accommodate sea-sailing ships and historic sailing ships that go to the Zuyder Zee, while salon boats must be able to tour. In a few years, the Central Station commuters will be able to transfer quickly from a train to an express boat, to go to a concert or a workshop located somewhere along the Ij.

New waterfront in La Habana Vieja

Havana is an anomaly in contemporary urban history. Its position in the 1950s, as an Antillean metropolis destined to become another nexus in the Las Vegas and Miami triangle of gambling and tourism, was frozen in time on January 1, 1959. Therefore, buildings and the urban fabric of Havana have withstood the encroachment of speculative urbanization. The overall plan of Havana comprises narrow, rectilinear streets organized according to an orthogonal grid. The development of the grid in the seventeenth century followed the Spanish urban guidelines set by the Law of the Indies. Before this, pragmatic concerns dictated development. The gridded plans of the New World represent a transition in European thinking from medieval to Renaissance planning. Typically, Hispano-American plans focus on a square with barracks, a *cabildo*, and a church. Havana, in contrast, made a square, Plaza Vieja, without the presence of church or

9.10 High-rise tower along the Malecón, Havana.

9.11 Plan for Havana, from the office of José Luis Sert.

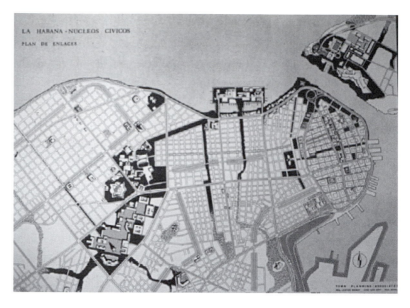

barracks and instead made a square for people and markets. A square based on commerce was rare for the time.

Baroque and neo-classical architecture constitute the fabric of the city. The cathedral and the important civic monuments, including the municipal palace of the eighteenth century, are of baroque inspiration, as are a number of other urban elements, including the Plaza Vieja. Neo-classical homes decorated with elaborate ironwork and arcades complement the fabric of the city. The architecture of old Havana represents five centuries of development, from the sixteenth to the twentieth centuries. Of the 900 historic buildings, 101 date from this century, 460 from last century, 200 from the eighteenth century and an astonishing 144 date from the seventeenth and sixteenth centuries.

The harbor and the remains of the old city walls define old Havana. The old city wall is two kilometers long and took 164 years to construct, lasting only sixty-six years. In the area defined by its circumference are more than fifty monuments and historic buildings of national and international importance. At the head of the harbor sits Castillo de la Punta, located at the junction of the Prado and Avienda Malecón, and across from it Castillo del Morro. The harbor barrier chain was strung between the two fortifications. Today the wharves and old warehouses, built to service the sea trade, still define the character of the harbor.

Of Havana's many features, some are worth noting. Havana is defined by four squares. Plaza de Armas and Plaza de la Catedral are the most important, but Plaza Vieja and Plaza de San Francisco are also of significance. Plaza de Armas is the oldest, situated at the seaward end of Calles O'Reilly and Obispo. The square contains the shrine of El Templete, commemorating the first Mass celebrated in Havana. It was the site of the first town council meeting in 1519. The square is where the Spanish governors ruled Havana from El Palacio de los Casa Bayona.

Plaza de la Catedral is a remarkable colonial entity in old Havana. It houses many historic buildings, including the baroque cathedral of San

Cristobal de la Habana, originally commissioned by the Jesuits and built from 1748 to 1777; El Palacio de los Condes Bayona, the oldest Spanish building on the square, built in 1720; the Marqueses de Arcos residence of 1741; the Palace of Conde Lombillo of 1587; and the palace of the Marqueses de Aguas Claras, who were descendants of Ponce de León who went to Florida looking for the Fountain of Youth.

After the Second World War, the city expanded west and southwest from the initial walled precinct. With this, the port and old Havana became less accessible and this condition worsened with the increase in motor vehicles. As Cuba industrialized after the war, several industrial complexes were constructed around the bay, including the oil refineries, dockyards, a gas plant, two oil-burning power stations, grain towers, cargo railways, a fertilizer plant, the piers along the southern half of old Havana, and a very large garbage dump called Cayo Cruz. The trade winds that once brought air to the city now brought smoke and foul odors from these assorted facilities.

The Master Plan of 1971 emphasized transportation and the construction of shipping terminals around the bay. It also proposed the expansion of port facilities to Matanzas, 100 kilometers east of Havana, and a better deep-water port, and also to Mariel, 45 kilometers west of the city. This dispersal of port activity would mean a consolidation of cargo and industry into a smaller area on the southern border of the bay, clearing the piers of old Havana so that the city could reconnect to the water. Because of the plan, several large port installations were built, including a fishing port. However, the old docks remained and continued to block the southern half of old Havana, in addition, the proposed Traffic Center, which would have removed the old railway terminal and reduced heavy traffic in the inner city, was never constructed.

In the mid-1990s, tourism became a significant source of revenue for Cuba. In response the city renovated one of the three main piers at the Custom Building and turned it into a cruise ship terminal. The success of this project increased the efforts of the City Historian's Office to restore many landmark buildings and plazas in old Havana. The Master Plan for the Comprehensive Revitalization of Old Havana was set up at the end of 1994, at the request of the City Historian's Office. The intention of the plan was to study the problems of the historic center and propose the best alternatives for its renovation. The Spanish Agency for International Cooperation was a consultant and partial financial supporter of these initiatives.

In 1994, the City Historian's Office was granted the special privilege, by the Council of State of the Republic of Cuba, to run businesses and reinvest profits in their own redevelopment and restoration programs, which now includes social programs aimed at improving the living conditions of the local population. The Office is concerned with more than just the physical preservation of Havana. It is engaged in the promotion of the city and the sympathetic commercial potential of the historic center. The historic center has produced more than 70 million dollars in five years (1999). In this period, 95 restoration projects were completed, 58 are underway and 79 more are being planned. The Office's programs are now completely self-financed.

As part of the comprehensive plan, several Autonomous Communities

9.12 View across Havana bay.

of the Spanish State, the City Historian's Office and the City of Havana Assembly of People Power, have joined in an effort to rehabilitate the first part of the Malecón from Paseo del Prado to Belascoain Street in Maceo Park. These fourteen blocks are mostly residential with some hotel, office and warehouse structures. The potential of this stretch of waterfront is tremendous; however, there are significant obstacles that need addressing. These problems include the state of the fabric, the role of the Malecón as a major transport artery, the lack of infrastructure, the deterioration wrought by salt water, and the quality of the water in the bay. The location of this stretch of the Malecón is ideal for commercial development; however, the condition of the existing fabric prohibits new uses and any such development must be in balance with the residential character of the area. Any new construction will be required to follow the general character of the existing fabric and maintain the rhythms of the traditional elements – ground floor, doorways, balconies, terraces, cornices, terraced roof, etc.

Until now, the cautious acceptance of Cuban–foreign tourist-related, real estate joint ventures, has concentrated on the best locations along the Malecón and in Miramar. This is despite attempts to redirect some of this development to the east, to large tracts of well-connected empty land. The problem is that even if these planning attempts may seem perfectly reasonable, they fly in the face of five centuries of development tradition.

Once the docks are gone from the southern part of the bay, some very interesting possibilities present themselves. It would allow, for example, the opening of the old walled precinct of the city to the water, and the recycling of the piers for commercial and leisure uses. This will allow for the public green spaces, related to the revitalization of the Alameda de Paula, to include things such as seafood restaurants, art galleries and shops. It would also allow the provision of boat tours around the bay or to nearby places such as Cojímar.

On the eastern part of the bay lies Casablanca, a small village that creeps over the top of a steep hill dominated by the huge La Cabaña fortress. A new waterfront promenade will create a new face for Casablanca and link the village to the water. This may include a new marina at Dársena de los Franceses, ending at the historic Batería de La Divina Pastora. Connections vertically up the hill would allow access to El Cristo de la Habana, a giant statue of Jesus Christ, and the weather observatory, which may be recycled into a planetarium.

A 300-year-old colonial town called Regla protrudes as a peninsula from the southern edge of the bay. Regla has a strong local character owing to its Afro-Cuban religion. A sea shuttle links Regla and Casablanca to Havana. At the ferry landing in Casablanca is the world's oldest operating electric tram. First commissioned in 1916, the tram connects Havana with Matanzas.

Havana bay has suffered from environmental pollution for some time. Currently there is a program with the United Nations Development Program/Global Environment Facility (UNDP/GEF) to reduce water pollution in the bay. The UNDP/GEF pilot phase project, "Planning and Management of Heavily Contaminated Bays and Coastal Areas in the Wider Caribbean," was a Pre-investment Facility (PRIF) project that dealt with Havana bay, Cuba; Cartagena bay, Colombia; Puerto Limón, Costa Rica; and Kingston harbor, Jamaica. Urban and industrial developments surround Havana bay, and these have a major impact on water quality. The bay receives suspended solids, hydrocarbons, heavy metals and other micro-pollutants from agriculture, industry and port activities. Havana's collection system does not treat the wastewater. Today many sewers discharge to local rivers flowing through the city. The tributary area of Havana bay, including the rivers Luyano and Martin Perez, receives polluted water from large residential areas and from some industrial areas. The project determined that the main sources of pollution are the Luyano River (organic material, nutrients, sewage, solid waste), the gas plant and the oil refinery, the Regla and Hacendados fish factories, and the fishing port.

9.13 The mouth of Havana harbor.

The government of Cuba has taken some mitigation measures to rehabilitate Havana bay, but the special economic situation in Cuba has limited its capacity. Cuba has several ongoing development programs for alternative, environmentally sound technologies related to wastewater treatment. The economic situation in Cuba also accentuates the need for potential domestic production of fertilizers and energy recovered from alternative wastewater treatment. In response to these needs, a new integrated sewage treatment plant will be constructed in eastern Havana to cover a population of about 57,000 in the Luyano River area. The plant will include nutrient removal and will allow for sludge utilization to energy or fertilizer.

In central Havana, the City Historian's Office, with help from several Spanish communities, is rehabilitating the oldest strip of the Malecón. The challenge of this work is how to invest economic life in the area, ensure self-sufficiency and balance the needs of development with current residents. Another challenge is how to slow down traffic on the Malecón, which currently is the fastest access to old Havana and the bay tunnel, so that pedestrians might gain access to the water's edge. Several projects to protect the front line of eclectic buildings from the rough winter sea or occasional tidal waves have been developed; however, such schemes require significant investment and are therefore hard to implement.

A well-defined triangular shaped neighborhood, La Fragua, lies between Centro Habana and La Rampa, the city's most lively mixed-use area from the 1950s and 1960s. The revitalization of La Fragua will improve the link between Centro Habana and Vedado and activate that strip of waterfront. This revitalization will involve the rehabilitation of a major historic axis in Havana, leading to Havana University, San Lázaro. The potential of this axis is tremendous. The northern part will allow more active development and one day will become the new La Rampa.

In eastern Havana, a historic park, Morro-Cabaña, is slowly being redeveloped. The area is rich with archeological material left by the Colonial military garrisons. Once complete, the waterfront park will provide the only nearby open space for residents in old Havana. Farther east, several new subdivisions might be developed, using some of the infrastructure from pre-revolutionary days. Eastern Havana has the benefits of clean air, fine sandy beaches and good connections to the city center. Planners in Havana see development in this area as essential to correct the imbalance of a city that grew west away from the original settlement beside the port. One area of particular interest is the small fishing village of Cojímar. It was here that Ernest Hemingway stored his fishing boat. Cojímar has a small colonial fort dating from 1646, located at the mouth of a river.

The prime piece of Havana waterfront is the Malecón. The Malecón waterfront is almost seven kilometers long and links old Havana with the west through Centro Habana and Vedado. Issues of preservation and the appropriateness of development are critical on the Malecón. It was here that Sert proposed his massive intervention, which would have significantly altered the character of the Malecón skyline. Planning authorities are currently studying the area to understand if high-rise development is appropriate. The issue, given the historic nature of the area, is how new commercial developments might situate themselves within the fabric of the city.

9.14 The Malecón, Havana.

The Malecón stops at the mouth of the Almendares River, Havana's main waterway. At the mouth of the Almendares is a small colonial fort, called La Chorrera, built in 1646. Currently there is a shantytown and an informal shipyard immediately adjacent to La Chorrera. Planning authorities in Havana are currently examining the possibility of relocating the shantytown dwellers and creating a park and marina in this location. The park and marina would be an extension of the Metropolitan Park currently under construction. This would allow for the continuation of the Malecón to the Vedado neighborhood. The development would be financed by income generated by new real estate investments in what would undoubtedly become one of Havana's prime locations.

9.15 Along the Malecón, Havana.

Slightly further to the west is Playa de Mariano where, prior to the Revolution, most of the private clubs were located. Playa de Mariano is located on a short crescent-shaped artificial beach and now is mostly used by trade union workers as a recreation spot. The area has tremendous potential for redevelopment in the new Cuba. A nearby military airport, no longer in service, would provide the largest redevelopment area west of Havana. This would link Playa de Mariano, and the once fashionable subdivision, with the working-class neighborhoods to the south, and provide a more direct connection to the international airport. Such projects would relieve some of the development pressure from the historic center of old Havana.

Conclusion

The comparison between Amsterdam and Havana provides us with an opportunity to explore the nature of waterfront development in historic cities. Amsterdam is a city with a long history of waterfront redevelopment, while Havana is just beginning its venture. Amsterdam is a city that can provide important lessons for how to deal with the difficult coming together of development and preservation.

Of particular interest are the lessons learned through the experience of the Amsterdam Waterfront Finance Company (AWF). One lesson is not to rely on a single market sector. Diversification allows for flexibility in the planning and execution of large-scale projects. It also allows for strategic integration into historic fabric. The fact that Amsterdam executes its

9.16 Close-up of the new Metropolis Museum, Amsterdam.

9.17 La Fragua, Havana.

waterfront redevelopment in the absence of a comprehensive plan is radical in that it suggests a more precise role for planning and design. Given the nature of contemporary society such precision is a way to guarantee a greater rate of success. It also allows for integration of old character with new expression.

Amsterdam is also remarkable for its acceptance of new expression in the architecture of its waterfront development. In North America, we have an obsessive desire for everything to be the same, to reduce everything to the lowest common denominator. Modern development must obey strict guide-

9.18 Boats in Amsterdam.

lines so as not to be offensive, expressive or unique. In our search for the contextual, we deny the possibility of new expressions. Amsterdam provides us with a different attitude, an alternative. This attitude allows for new ways of thinking about the cultural production of space and the role of heritage in that production. Contextualism, in this sense, is not about the reproduction of the old but about the ability of the new to make relationships with the old. The new can make us aware of the old in new and exciting ways.

In Havana these issues are critical and pressing. What Havana needs is a way to conceptualize the identity of the city in such a manner as to prioritize the manipulation of the old fabric and the integration of the new. This would be well served by small-scale incremental approaches to the development of the city. Approaches that would suit the economic reality of Cuba and be flexible enough to adapt to changing circumstances.

"Waterfronts, development and World Heritage cities" was based in part upon case material prepared by researchers at the Harvard Design School and presentations by Professor Mario Coyula, Director, Grupo para el Desarrollo Integral de la Capital, Havana, Cuba, and Alderman Duco Stadig, Alderman of Public Housing, Urban Renewal and Urban Planning, Real Estate Affairs and Development of the Ij-embankment, Amsterdam, at the Waterfronts in Post Industrial Cities Conference, 7–9 October, 1999, Harvard Design School, Cambridge, Massachusetts.

References

Aben, R. (1998a) "Stationeiland," *PlanAmsterdam*, 4 (2), February.

Aben, R. (1998b) "Rails aan het Ij," *PlanAmsterdam*, 4 (8), October.

Amsterdam Bureau for Research and Statistics (1998) *Key Figures: Amsterdam 1998*, July.

Amsterdam Economic Development Department (1999a) *Amsterdam: Portraits of a Versatile City*, Amsterdam Promotion Foundation.

Amsterdam Economic Development Department (1999b) *The Attractions and Dimensions of Greater Amsterdam*.

Amsterdam Economic Development Department (1999c) *Facts and Figures of the Greater Amsterdam Area*.

Barclay, J. (1993) *Havana: Portrait of a City*, London: Cassell.

Berry, J. and McGreal, S. (eds) (1995) *European Cities, Planning Systems and Property Markets*, London: Spon.

CiudadCity (1997) The Havanan Malecón: A Transformation and Cooperation Process, Programa Malecón, España + Cuba, Revitalización Integral de La Habana Vieja.

CiudadCity (1999) Challenge of a Utopia: A Comprehensive Strategy to Manage the Safeguarding of the Old Havana, Oficina del Historiador de la Ciudad de la Habana, Revitalización Integral de La Habana Vieja.

Gravette, A.G. (1988) *Cuba Official Guide*, London and Basingstoke: Macmillan Caribbean.

http://www.amsterdam.nl

http://www.havanaport.com

http://www.ovpm.org/ovpm/sites/ahavan.html

Karst, J. (1998) "Water en Land maken Ijburg," *PlanAmsterdam*, 4 (3), March.

de Laat, Leon (1997) "Open Stad: Structuurplan Amsterdam 1996 vastesteld," *PlanAmsterdam*, 3 (4), May.

de Lang and Schaap (1995), "Borneo en Sporenburg een nieuwe wijk in het Oostelijk Havengebied," *PlanAmsterdam*, 1 (2), April.

Malone, P. (ed.) (1996) *City, Capital and Water*, London and New York: Routledge.

Meyer, H. (1999) *City and Port: Urban Planning as a Cultural Venture in London, Barcelona, New York, and Rotterdam*, Utrecht, The Netherlands: International Books.

Michener, J. and Kings, J. (1989) *Six Days in Havana*, Austin: University of Texas Press.

Municipality of Amsterdam (1999) *Amsterdam Develops: Ij-oevers Amsterdam On the Ij*, Amsterdam.

Pistor, R. (ed.) (1994) *A City in Progress: Physical Planning in Amsterdam*, Amsterdam: Dienst Ruimtelijke Ordening Amsterdam.

Sapieh, N. (1990) *Old Havana, Cuba*, London: Tauris Parke Books.

Serge, R., Coyula, M., and Scarpaci, J. (1997) *Havana: Two Faces of the Antillean Metropolis*, New York: John Wiley and Sons.

Schaap, T. (1998) "Stads Arcadie," *PlanAmsterdam*, 4 (5/6), May/June.

Stout, N. and Rigau, J. (1994) *La Habana*, New York: Rizzoli.

10 History at the water's edge

Barry Shaw

Introduction

Ideas in planning and architecture have traditionally taken around thirty years to go from being radical and experimental to becoming the accepted norm, from being argued in political, professional and academic institutions to becoming the textbook methodology. The first stage in the process belongs to the visionaries able to offer new insight that somehow captures the *Zeitgeist*. They are followed at the second stage by the developers who expand the idea, often finding a broader application. During the third stage the idea is so widely accepted that it becomes standard practice. At this point of general recognition the idea is often discarded or radically altered by a new generation who, through hindsight and analysis, are once again able to respond to further change in an original way. Baltimore Inner Harbor was the largest of this first generation of waterfront redevelopments. It was followed by two rapid and overlapping generations of development that also saw the ideas taken up internationally. The fourth generation of rethinkers should now be emerging.

The popularity of waterfront development owes much to the fact that virtually every city has a downtown waterfront that offers a mix of scales and uses close to the center, offering an urban quality while at the same time providing new development opportunity. Water, the primary human resource, was the reason for the original location, providing means of transport, defense, leisure and recreation. But it was not just the physical form of the old harbors that influenced so much subsequent planning. Old industries had gathered on land that was not wanted and was cheap. There is also an emotive link with historical development that shaped so many lives and influenced the culture of cities. The fact that most industrial cities had turned their backs on their waterfronts for so long meant there was an element of rediscovery and emotional re-engagement. This first generation of waterfront transformations succeeded because they changed the problem scenario of redundant waterfront industry into one of opportunity.

Growing wealth, growing populations and increased leisure time enabled a new generation of leisure-oriented developments, often using the historical associations as a form of brand image. The architecture of these new building types developed out of pioneering conservation projects that successfully adapted former industrial buildings to commercial use. Projects such as Boston's Fanieul Market Place and San Francisco's Ghiradelli Square had highlighted public sentiment for their local heritage, in contrast to the prevailing neutral internationalism of city development.

The projects were created at city scale, large enough to have an impact on a big derelict area. They became a unifying symbol for city dwellers, who were able to identify with the new/old neighborhoods rather than the declining whole. The underlying aim was to lift the self-image of areas of cities formally associated with decay and failure and to underpin a fresh optimism with popular new development. The waterfront was recognized as "the missing ingredient" which made it all work as one. Instead of a series of attractions there was the continuity of the waterfront shoreline with a rich history of development and association.

Historic preservation and waterfront development

With hindsight the challenges look much less daunting than they were to the pioneers of waterfront redevelopment. In the 1970s nobody knew how to go about protecting large bodies of water and big industrial complexes. The conservation of a large-scale landscape of dock buildings and industrial waterscapes required new development strategies. The physical challenges of individual structures were difficult to assess as the sites were often developed on marsh or reclaimed land with foundations that were not to contemporary standards. Harbor walls and service infrastructures had been designed for different purposes and were in many cases time-expired. The historic waterfront comprised not only buildings, but also structures, dock walls, historic artifacts and signs of different materials and periods. Below ground was an infrastructure assembled in a way that reflected former work practices and original topographical features. Hidden from view were the legal issues, such as rights of access, and liabilities of many sorts. There were often complex patterns of division with multiple leases and assemblies of small parcels of land and property in different ownerships. The potential for new use was affected by changing standards of safety in the workplace, of what constituted a hazard or a pollutant and the physical ability of the original structures to take change.

There was the need to find new uses appropriate to buildings designated as historic structures. Accommodating the car, together with access for modern services, was a major problem. More generally there was a need to assemble a range of facilities to attract and service the new users. New uses brought with them their own standards and regulations ranging from levels of natural light to fire protection and means of escape. The financial uncertainty of not knowing exactly what would be found when a structure was altered was increased by the difficulty of predicting the level of demand for a type of property that had not previously been marketed. The marketability of the location was affected by the provision of new infrastructure and services that were the responsibility of other service providers, often with their own budget problems and priorities.

A clear view of what constituted historic fabric or a historic area was not always easy to produce. Most structures did not match existing definitions of the historic. The character of small, compact historic areas was relatively easy to define, but that of large industrial estates was very different. The conservation process was itself uncertain. One of the arts of large-scale conservation was to know when to allow demolition and when to fight for preservation.

More intransigent were the legal problems of liability that arose when land or buildings were transferred or their uses changed. A century or more of the industrial management of the harbors and their associated industrial estates had created complex boundaries and responsibilities. The harbor authorities were often organizations that had not come to terms with the decline of their industry and wanted to preserve the area as a working dock with rights of access that were no longer appropriate. Alternatively the various industrial owners saw an opportunity to make money out of assets they had previously seen as valueless. By waiting and doing nothing they stood to profit from the general improvement. But by not allowing development they could reduce the impact of those schemes that were able to start, and by continuing with low-value uses they could detract from area-wide change.

It required a considerable rise in the value of land to give a financial return that could cover the cost of retention and restoration. The established development industry was risk-averse, preferring to demolish what was there and to replace it with new construction. In many cases the local building industry lacked the skill required to work with old structures on so large a scale. Many of the early successes relied on a few farsighted individuals with the skills and tenacity to bring about their vision, such as Rouse in Baltimore and Boston, or Wadsworth in London.

Four generations of urban waterfront development

The progenitors for first-generation Baltimore emerged from relatively wealthy cities that had retained much of their historic fabric. The successful initial transformations of industrial buildings in prominent waterfronts were sensitive and, for their time, radical restorations of fabric which was often scheduled for demolition. In 1965, in San Francisco, Lawrence Halprin & Associates, working with urban designers Bernardi and Emmons, created Ghiradelli Square, a new public space facing the bay against the backdrop of a former chocolate factory with the adjacent former cannery building forming a sophisticated retailing facility. The restoration of Faneuil Hall Marketplace reversed the decline of Boston's downtown area. London's Covent Garden, although not on the waterfront, was another landmark in conservation brought about by public pressure led by radical professionals.

These schemes marked a revival of urbanism after the postwar decades of flight from the city. They were also the beginning of a rejection of what was seen as orthodox modern architecture that had failed to create a sense of place and failed to pay sufficient creative attention to the design of the urban fabric. There was a growing awareness of the value and usefulness of heritage and a reaffirmation of local and national identity in the face of the challenges of globalization.

It is twenty years since what is generally recognized as the first of the modern waterfronts was opened in Baltimore in July 1980. The city's Inner Harbor Renewal Plan was seen as providing an innovative solution and fresh impetus to the problem of inner city decay that characterized the beginning of the post-industrial period. It remains one of the most complete examples. The reclamation of the waterfront has subsequently become a symbol of post-industrial status. In the global economy of the information age they offer the opportunity to signal national and local identity. And like other competitive global products they have developed a structure that is pretty well universally applicable while at the same time capable of being adapted for local consumption.

Baltimore, seen as a national symbol of decay, had been working on its downtown plan for fifteen years (Baltimore City Department of Planning, 1986). The city brought together most of the characteristic elements of waterfront development. The authorities recognized that the problem was of a scale too large for the private sector alone to take on and sanctioned the heavy use of public funds as seed money for private investment. The project was managed by an unusually centralized city government that had merged neighborhood and economic development into one department. It was led by a far-seeing and energetic director working in tandem with an equally committed and powerful mayor. The initial focus was on the downtown area. The subsequent continuation of development reclaimed the waterfront with a series of "flagship" projects starting with the Harborplace festival-market development and a new aquarium. High-quality infrastructure around much of the inner harbor opened up what had been private and inaccessible, enabled access to the community for a wide variety of uses that embedded the area in local consciousness, and so attracted further development. The range of issues and the balance between old and new was set out in contemporary documents:

> Millions of public and private dollars are committed to keep the Port competitive and to enhance its stance in the international marketplace money. There are also plans which call for rehabilitating commercial properties, converting vacant warehouses and building new housing, improving the water quality, and increasing the recreational use of the shoreline and water.
>
> (Baltimore City Department of Planning, 1986)

The second generation

The second generation of post-industrial waterfronts was led by organizations that were set up specifically to develop their waterfront area, building on, testing, and expanding the package of measures pioneered in Baltimore. These developments mostly belonged to the 1980s and some even came to characterize that decade. Boston was a key player in this second wave just as it had been inspirational in the first, with the establishment of the Boston Redevelopment Authority (BRA) as a dedicated multidisciplinary body charged solely with the task of regenerating the Charlestown Harbor area of the city. It was a global movement with influential projects in Darling Harbour in Sydney, Australia; in Toronto, Canada; and in Cape Town, South Africa.

But it was in Europe that the idea of a second generation was developed, brought about by the scale required of renewal in cities like London and Barcelona, which was sub-regional and, arguably, sub-national in scope. European planning and city management had a different culture compared to North American cities. Public ownership of land, of many of the old industrial utilities and most particularly of social housing, separated private investment from public programmes. With the general exception of the downtown areas the public sector was traditionally responsible for planning and funding inner city building programmes. These second wave projects helped develop a new approach with the creation of public–private partnerships and the extensive use of private investment.

The London Docklands Development Corporation (LDDC) was established in 1980 following national legislation that also enabled the transfer of land from other public bodies such as the ports authority, together with the granting of development control (planning) powers transferred from the local authorities. It was charged with the regeneration of eight square miles of former docks. In embracing North American style urban renewal the British government sought to ensure that the private sector would play a leading role in shaping and delivering the program. The task was seen to be too expensive for the public sector alone and required not only active investment but also the development know-how of the private sector. The Corporation was given extensive powers and was freed from local accountability. This approach was regarded as overtly political and fought against by local politicians who were given, with few exceptions, little say in the process. It was a time of polarized opinions.

Public/social housing was the most visible element of the change in policy. It was replaced as the lead development ingredient by private housing. The notion of fully funded public estates was displaced by the idea of "affordable housing." Effectively it was a subsidy whereby a percentage of property, initially 25–30 percent, on private developments was subsidized, usually out of land value. It also sought to entice the volume builders (private house builders) back to the old inner city areas after a gap of nearly one hundred years. London, like most European cities, had developed a strong tradition of providing public housing for the working classes, with the public sector owning as much as 96 percent of all the housing in the LDDC development area.

London also highlighted the role of planning. Top-down, plan-led, public sector planner-led development was seen as having failed the inner city during the 1960s and 1970s. This led to the questioning of the traditional overall Master Plan blueprint for development in favor of more flexible development plans which were quick to bring about and easier to change. The process was seen to be dynamic, not static. There was pressure of time and money, and in particular the need to be realistic about what was possible and could be afforded. Working closely with the private sector required good negotiating skills as well as good planning skills.

Another controversial element in London was the creation of Enterprise Zones. Targeted at attracting private businesses to the unfashionable East End the initiative consisted of demarcating an area of the development for industrial and office use and encouraging development through a series of tax incentives and, more controversially, the removal of planning restrictions. It was asserted that private "entrepreneurs" knew better than public sector planners where and how they place their scarce investments. Planning was seen by the government of the day as negative and culturally weighted in favor of traditional public sector values.

The LDDC was seen by some observers as having abandoned town planning. In fact it did not produce an overall Master Plan but rather a series of local plans, including a comprehensive conservation plan (London Docklands Development Corporation, 1987). These were considered more flexible and succeeded in achieving rapid and extensive development. More critically major investment in public infrastructure came late, with the new underground railway Jubilee Line extension opening nearly twenty years after the project was set up and just as the LDDC was closing down. One of the paradoxes of this debate was that what emerged was the highly "planned" Canary Wharf development, the largest of its type in Europe.

Conservation was planned, and strongly supported, for most of the life of the Corporation and was instrumental in establishing the new image of the Docklands. The 1970s in London had seen a major conservation success with the battle to save Covent Garden, but also significant failures – especially the destruction of the Telford warehouses at St Katharine's Dock and many Victorian warehouses at the London Docks. The London Docks had been drained and filled, as had much of the Surrey Docks. The local authorities were ambivalent about the Docklands heritage and there were no large-scale examples of successful conservation of nineteenth-century industrial structures on the scale of London Docklands.

The Docklands was not a homogeneous area with a single type of development. Conservation policies had to be developed for an area extending over some eight square miles with an enormous diversity of building types and periods. For nearly 2,000 years London had owed its commercial pre-eminence to the Thames that allowed a major port to develop some forty miles inland, and intensive waterfront development had left an unusually rich heritage, although what remained visible represented only the last two centuries. Extensive Roman and medieval quays had been excavated in the city beyond the LDDC boundary of operation. Within the Docklands area one of the oldest remaining large structures, although altered beyond recognition, was the enclosed dock at Howland Quay dating from 1699, and later expanded and renamed Greenland Dock. Much more complete were the West India Docks (1799–1806), the London Docks (1800–1805), and the East India Docks (1803–1806) as well as St Katharine's Dock (1825–1828).

The development of railways and steamships toward the latter part of the nineteenth century had brought about a new form of dock at a much larger scale, and correspondingly further out from the city in what became known as the Royal Docks, built between 1850 (Royal Victoria Dock) to 1921 with the completion of the King George V Docks. The dates refer to the main building projects; a study of maps of London shows that the whole Docklands area underwent more or less continuous development up until the end of the Second World War. Most of the early docks closed in the 1960s, with the Royal group finally closing in 1981. Severe damage during the Second World War, and extensive demolition in the postwar period, left a scattered pattern of historical structures.

The oldest areas were the riverside wharves that stretched from Black-friars, north of the Thames, to Limehouse; Rotherhithe on the south bank had also declined badly. By 1981 they were all in a poor state of repair. Significant clusters of mostly nineteenth-century brick warehouses remained in Wapping, Rotherhithe, and along a stretch running from Clink Street to St Saviours Dock and Shad Thames. Around these wharves there remained working communities, housed for the most part in public housing built in the 1920s, 1930s, 1950s and 1960s. Within these areas was a different heritage, most significant of which were the churches dating from the seventeenth and eighteenth centuries.

The Local Government Land and Planning Act 1980 defined the powers of the LDDC as follows. "The object of an Urban Development Corporation shall be to secure . . . regeneration . . . by bringing land and buildings into effective use . . ." Thus regeneration was explicitly to involve bringing into use obsolete buildings, including those of historic importance, and the protection and enhancement of conservation areas. The Docklands developed an approach that was activity led. Rather than wait to draw up formal strategies the LDDC assembled a development planning team with strong landscaping and conservation skills. The most important conservation decision was to retain all the remaining water areas that distinguished the area from other parts of East London. The remaining docks were repaired. Large areas of filled dock were re-excavated in Wapping, Surrey and Greenland Docks. Where it was impracticable to restore large areas of water new canals were created to preserve the character of the remaining structures. These new water features provided continuity of hard landscaping and water flow, but also a substantial link with the Docklands heritage. They were at a scale large enough to have an impact over a big area and designed to utilize remaining features, such as locks and fragments of quayside, and extensively finished with reclaimed materials.

Only a small proportion of the buildings and structures of the Docklands were listed, but they were among the most distinctive and valued. The incorporation of buildings in the Statutory List made it unlawful to demolish or alter without Listed Building Consent. The criteria for listing covered four groups of building type:

1 all buildings built before 1700 which survive in anything like their original condition;
2 most buildings of between 1700 and 1840 (though selection is necessary);
3 buildings of definite quality and character built between 1840 and 1914; and
4 a limited number of buildings of high quality designed between 1914 and 1939.

It was recognized early on that the opening up of the dock areas would bring to light many buildings and structures worthy of listing. The Corporation successfully made a case for the listing of an additional 116 buildings as being of special historic interest and followed this initial move with further listings as more buildings were rediscovered. It inherited ten conservation areas in 1981, two of which it extended and a further seven designated. Key artifacts, such as the cranes, were purchased and preserved. The first buildings to be restored were the Docklands churches. The cleaning and repairing of Nicholas Hawksmoor's St George in the East and St Anne's Limehouse were early indicators of an area about to be changed, but were nevertheless controversial as it was considered by many local organizations that the money should have gone into new social facilities rather than old buildings.

Warehouse restoration followed, with extensive early conversions happening in Wapping, the area of Docklands closest to the city. These too were initially controversial, as many felt they would rather see them demolished to make way for new uses. In one week over fifty fires were reported in empty warehouses. Some of the restorations could more accurately be called resuscitations, with structures such as the Old Skin Floor buildings at Tobacco Dock being rebuilt for retailing use to a standard of restoration that must have exceeded the original quality of the building. Structures such as dock walls were also retained, maintaining fragments of previous land patterns to which new building was forced to relate to.

In some of the most difficult areas, such as the Shad Thames area around Tower Bridge, the density of warehouse building initially defied reuse. The building regulations were not flexible enough to allow for the retention of cast iron columns and timber floors that were regarded as a fire hazard. The size of buildings such as the Butlers Wharf warehouse made them initially unattractive even to those developers prepared to work with old structures. However, gradually by example, the technical problems were solved and the steady build up of cleaned and restored structures acted as a catalyst for the restoration of the entire area.

Shad Thames is a long, narrow, winding Thameside street and one of the few surviving waterfront communities that used to characterize London's Dockland before the nineteenth-century expansion eastward beyond the original city boundaries. With other surviving areas in Rotherhithe, Wapping and Bankside it represented a pattern of development that was medieval in origin. The winding streets followed the line of the Thames and, although lined with tall nineteenth-century brick warehouses and other industrial structures, retained the informal, almost rustic, layout of an earlier period. The street has a strong urban quality and links a series of architecturally significant schemes ranging from the south piers of Tower Bridge to St Saviours Dock and Dockhead.

The decision was taken both to retain everything that could be retained and also to ensure that where new development occurred it should reflect the best of modern design. This approach extended beyond those buildings that were listed to include anything that could be said to preserve or enhance the area. Most critically it included the retention of the original geometry of the streets. It presented designers with a challenge. New buildings acknowledged, without replicating, the older, dense forms. The Vogans Mill development, for example, created a white tower constructed around the remains of a former grain silo. New office buildings at Saffron Wharf contrast with the adjacent dark brick. A new Design Museum was created out of a concrete-framed warehouse built in the 1940s.

The centerpiece of the area is the Butlers Wharf site, acquired relatively cheaply for less than £5 million in 1984 by a consortium led by Terence

Conran. The area contained an assortment of structures, of which seventeen were listed. Buildings of poor quality were demolished to allow for new development. The approach required flexibility, in part because it was argued that new development was required to provide financial support for the restoration of large difficult structures. Car parking was required in the area, and this was provided in spaces under the new buildings.

The uses could not be restored. The streets were too narrow for modern lorries, and with a few lingering exceptions, such as a delightfully fragrant spice mill, the uses became primarily residential and commercial. Mixed use is notoriously difficult to achieve with new development. The Butlers Wharf area was more successful than most in that it offered a wide variety of types of space, and, at least initially as the area was emerging, some variation in rental cost. A flexible approach was adopted to planning use consents, allowing some areas to change their use a number of times, oscillating between residential, commercial or retailing until such time as the area developed its own sense of place, about ten years after the first structures were converted. This at times controversial mix of new and old resulted in an area that has overwhelmingly retained its historic character while at the same time becoming a lively new city quarter known for its restaurants and creative industries.

The process of regeneration as it emerged in the Docklands was unusual in that it was superimposed on the local authorities, who were given a very limited say in what it did. Overall London produced a somewhat controversial development, elements of which were seen as a model to avoid as much as copy. Local opposition to the new waterfronts was a characteristic of the post-industrial nature of these projects, but it was particularly bitter in London. It succeeded, however, in transforming the approach to regeneration planning in the UK; in helping the development of a new approach to conservation; and by demonstrating that large-scale planning was economically viable.

Barcelona, in contrast to London, was architect-led and plan-led. It made full use of the opportunity presented by the 1992 Olympic Games being held in the city to develop a long-term integrated planning strategy. The first of its four basic objectives was the application of an urban structure aimed at creating a new area that was not alien in character or divorced from adjoining neighborhoods (Gili, 1988). The main contribution to the second generation of waterfront planning was the approach to infrastructure and the very clear support given not only to infrastructure-led development but also to rethinking the mistakes of the past. Rotterdam was also a pathfinding second-generation development, characterized most strongly by a well-led approach to community development and adventurous architecture.

Cardiff, Liverpool, Salford, Berlin

It is a characteristic of the third generation that the ideas are tried and accepted and capable of being applied to smaller waterfront cities and towns as they are to the big cities. This generation is marked by the acceptance into the mainstream of development practice all the elements developed by the first two waves of waterfront regeneration. In Europe Cardiff Bay, Liverpool and Salford Docks are all succeeding, and Berlin's Wasserstadt is underway; in Australia Sydney and Perth have large successful developments, as does Vancouver in Canada. In Asia there is an explosion of city developments of which the largest is probably China's Shanghai.

Boston's inner city was the first step in a planning program known as "the walk to the sea." They owed much to a burgeoning dissatisfaction with the Modern Movement eloquently expressed by Jane Jacobs in the seminal *Death and Life of Great American Cities: The Failure of Town Planning* (Jacobs, 1961). These schemes recognized the value of old buildings as a symbol of community memory. Modern city planning had got it wrong. People needed old-fashioned streets and urban patterns.

The second generation of waterfronts recognized the need for subsidy from the public purse for extensive conservation programmes, but the cost of total preservation had to fight for prioritization with all the other elements such as transport infrastructure. The key to conservation in areas is time, but with failing structures this is not always available.

Amsterdam is notable for the breadth of its approach. "Taking the future with the past" allows cross subsidy for conservation from areas easier to develop. The public sector acquires the land and land ownership always reverts to the city, giving it great flexibility. Its level of public investment is high in recognition of the value to the city of high-quality refurbishment as well as new building. Amsterdam, like Boston, also created urban design regulations to provide continuity within a flexible framework. Elsewhere conservation planning has meant the protection of surviving fragments of history.

Overall it is a characteristic of waterfront development to display a positive approach to conservation. In many areas new development has taken the dominant role, tempered by an understanding of the history of the area, its topography, waterscape and remaining artifacts, both architectural and engineering. Positive planning policies have been introduced that encouraged the conservation of worthwhile buildings to suitable new uses. This approach needs to be supported by an incremental approach to the eradication of derelict empty buildings and low-grade uses. In the UK the designation of "conservation areas" provided the mechanism by which an area's historic fabric can be provided with additional planning controls that ensure that new buildings within the area respect their surroundings.

The success of conservation-led regeneration of the waterfront has led to a new phase of historic preservation and a different approach characterized as adaptive reuse. Building on existing assets creates sustainable development and recognizes the importance of character and diversity to identity and inclusion. This approach relies rather less on the historic exactitude and gives rather more weight to the economic and social arguments. In the UK the national body with responsibility for conservation, English Heritage, has begun to calculate the financial value of heritage investment. It has identified three themes that reflect the regeneration impact: investment in economic change and social inclusion; investment in quality and sustainability; and investment in people and communities through partnership (English Heritage, 1999). It has put a monetary value on conservation. A broad selection of thirty-one (non-waterfront) examples showed that the funding proportion was on average 1:5.8. For every £1 contributed by the heritage agency private and other public sector bodies contributed £5.8.

If reuse of historic fabric underpinned the post-industrial waterfront it would be too simplistic to see all conservation in the same way. Cities such as Amsterdam and Havana have retained great quantities of ancient fabric sufficient for them to be classed as World Heritage Sites. For these cities the conservation debate is about authenticity and the need to assimilate change without losing the essence of the place. Mechanisms to support conservation are required. Success depends on quality and sustainability, and on developing support for conservation. Conservation plans are required, together with integrated administrative structures capable of delivering the projects and strong enough to resist the temptation to cut corners and demolish.

The Venice Charter (ICOMOS, 1964) and subsequent Declaration of Amsterdam (ICOMOS, 1975) set the precedent and outlined the approach. The language of ICOMOS is very much the language of regeneration:

> Effective conservation policies require broad public support. And like any other idea or commodity, the worth of such policies may not be immediately self-evident to all groups without promotional effort. Conservation advocates who wish to see their message achieve higher levels of support may benefit from the analysis that marketing specialists bring to their work: a clear definition of the intended market, and clarification of the intended message. Conservation groups have not always managed to imbue their cause with strong appeal. While the environmental cause is couched in a friendly "green", heritage conservation is still perceived by many as a fringe activity. World heritage towns have begun to sell their cause according to sound marketing practices, as a part of the global good, to begin to combat this inadequacy.

Master plans

Most cities use master plans to suggest the preferred direction of growth and development within a prescribed future time period, and to provide a framework for restricting or channeling development proposals to conform to an overall vision. These are often accompanied by secondary plans, which provide greater detail on a sector-by-sector basis. But many cities, once having proclaimed their master plans, ignore them in practice. Master plans which provide exemption each time aggressive developments are proposed are of little real value in guiding decision-makers.

Historic cities, which take full advantage of the ability of the master plan to guide decisions, are likely to accompany such plans with the following:

- full participation of various interests within a city in development of the master plan;
- faithful and consistent adherence to the master plan in the face of development review applications;

- incorporation within the master plan of clearly delineated conservation plans, clarifying zones requiring special treatment, and the nature of that treatment.

Integrated administrative structures

Civic governments generally develop internal structures aligned with the particular services they deliver. Department heads, each responsible for a particular set of services, compete with each other for available resources to fulfill their respective mandates. Once heritage conservation is recognized by a civic administration as a legitimate field of endeavor, those responsible are usually housed within a city's planning department, since it is principally through the use of planning mechanisms that cities involve themselves in conservation.

As long as heritage conservation is perceived as a "service," its capacity to influence will be limited by the strength of the particular voices or departments championing its worth in civic debate. Increasing the size of the conservation unit department is therefore not the only means to increase the acceptance of conservation ideas; nor is the creation of special heritage units to coordinate conservation activities and goals among departments. Indeed, in the long run, recognizing conservation as a legitimate civic objective, it may be more useful to promote appropriate "attitudes" within other departments.

Conclusion: the fourth generation

The fourth generation, the emerging wave, is being led by cities such as Amsterdam. Starting their developments in the aftermath of the 1990s world-wide economic recession, they are having to rethink the use of resources. Learning from its own earlier proposals for the Ij, Amsterdam is also rethinking the key components of architecture as a part of city building. The idea of the post-industrial city is a transitional one, appropriate perhaps to turn-of-the-century uncertainty. The character of the post-industrial waterfront in the information age is not yet clear. As we enter the twenty-first century there is a sense of celebration. What we expect is that the balance between cultural opportunity and quality of life will play a dominant part in shaping the successful city.

With waterfront development it has often been the case that theory has followed practice, the main forums for discussion being the conferences that have brought together practitioners. It is to be hoped that the Harvard Conference may mark the beginning of a radical review by a new generation better able to see the needs of the information age.

References

Baltimore City Department of Planning (1986) *The Baltimore Harbor*, Baltimore, MD.

English Heritage (1999) *The Heritage Dividend*, London.

Gili, Gustavo (1988) Martorell Bohigas Mackay Puigdomenech, *Transformation of a Seafront*, S.A., Barcelona.

ICOMOS (1964) *The Venice Charter*.

ICOMOS (1975) *The Declaration of Amsterdam*.

Jacobs, Jane (1961) *The Death and Life of Great American Cities: The Failure of Town Planning*, New York: Random House.

London Docklands Development Corporation (1987) *Docklands Heritage*, London

William Donald Schaefer, Mayor, City of Baltimore (1986) "The Baltimore Harbor," Baltimore City Department of Planning, Baltimore, MD.

11 Reflections on the Boston waterfront

Alex Krieger

As it has done several times over its 370-year history, the city of Boston is in the midst of redesigning one of its waterfronts. The newly renamed South Boston Seaport District, an area exceeding 700 acres in size and lying directly east of the center of the city, is poised to receive the next expansion of the downtown. Amidst a robust economy and following substantial public investment in regional access, including a new harbor tunnel which brings the airport to the district's doorstep, the Seaport District is brimming with anticipation – with plans, investors, visions – although there are ample worries and political intrigue.

Such a combination of hope and unease is common today among waterfront cities around the world since often it is along their waterfronts that major planning and redevelopment – or expectation that there a repositioning of local economies is possible – is taking place.

The impending reuse of an urban waterfront generally combines grand expectations with considerable self-reflection about the very nature of contemporary urbanism. Should planning for reuse support traditional maritime industries or promote new economies? Should cities seek new markets/status through refurbished waterfronts or maintain long-standing identities? Should public investment favor residents' needs, attract newcomers or cater to tourists; should it be used to shore-up adjoining neighborhoods or encourage gentrification; increase public access or leverage private development at water's edge? Should commercial expansion be favored or multiple civic needs addressed, especially those which private initiative does not readily achieve? Should, for example, cities seek to profit from the scale of modern development attracted to reconnected waterfronts or restrict density while enlarging recreational space?

Wise waterfront planning seeks to unravel such unnecessarily polarized visions. Yet, despite more than a decade of planning, if halting public decision-making, the unraveling of polarized visions over Boston's Seaport District remains, at the time of the writing of this chapter, incomplete.

Boston's Seaport District

The area encompassing the Seaport District was created a century ago through a massive landfill initiative. The goal was the creation of a modern boat-to-rail port to replace the historic but by then obsolete central piers of Boston, no longer able to accommodate the scale of modern ships and lacking sufficient rail connections. However, since the decline of local maritime industries which began shortly following the First World War, the area has been underutilized, maintaining some maritime and industrial functions but also hosting large parking fields and similar supporting uses for the nearby downtown. The area has essentially served as a land bank for years, awaiting better regional access and, more importantly, demand for the expansion of the nearby downtown.

Suddenly, seemingly overnight, it is metamorphizing into convention venues, hotels, luxury housing, parks and a cultural amenity or two. But some wonder if there will still be room for the traditional fishing fleet once such a fabulous array of modern uses – upwards of twenty million square feet are in various stages of planning or design – are realized. And the concern is not just about the survival of the fishing fleet, itself diminished over the years with the depletion of nearby fishing banks. The concerns extend to feared overbuilding, traffic congestion, gentrification and affordability, particularly of the housing being proposed, and the long-term affects on the cohesiveness (and some would say parochialism) of the adjacent South Boston community, long a cohesive working-class neighborhood, largely of Irish-American make-up and generally intolerant of outsider influence. Maintaining industrial jobs for the residents of South Boston is another concern. Other worries include whether sufficient public space will be provided, whether the right balance of uses are being planned, whether the public sector can sufficiently guide the actions of a few large and powerful landowners, whether too much history will be erased, who stands to gain or lose local political influence, and so forth.

Somehow, two centuries of producing new waterfronts – each a radical undertaking for its day, each eschewing conventional wisdom or timidity, each producing a quite striking and distinct environment – haven't produced a confidence about doing it well at the Seaport District. Before returning to the current dilemmas at the Seaport District, it is worth a brief review of Boston's waterfront planning achievements and to seek insights from the experience of the eight cities which presented their waterfront plans at the Harvard conference.

Boston's waterfront-making history

The story of Boston's waterfront planning begins with the city's remarkable topographic transformations. Few of the world's cities, large or small (with the possible exception of contemporary Hong Kong), have witnessed as substantial a change to their natural geographies as has Boston. As one walks around central Boston it is nearly impossible to visualize that the original Shawmut Peninsula was virtually an island, and that four out of five acres at one's feet is artificial land, constructed out of the determination to grow and prosper amidst a geography of steep hills, tidal flats, marshes and areas of usable land too meager in size to support any sizeable settlement. To accommodate growth the city would have no choice but to make land. From the early decades of the eighteenth century an expanding seafaring economy led the young city to push outward into its harbors and bays to gain usable land.

The process began in two ways: by "wharfing out" – the filling of the slips of water between wharves – and with the dumping of earth into the harbor from the scraping of the steepest hills to make them easier to settle. These efforts foreshadowed the much larger nineteenth-century land-making ventures out of which emerged the form of contemporary Boston. The earliest recorded filling, for the purpose of adding usable land rather than as a mere consequence of clearing existing areas for settlement, occurred in 1803 with the widening of the peninsula neck, generally parallel to today's Washington Street. Rapidly following were the filling of portions of the West Cove (the area around the present Massachusetts General Hospital), and the Mill Pond which became the Bullfinch Triangle. Early nineteenth-century maps of Boston depict these expansions well, on the eve of the most famous land-making project – the nearly 600-acre filling of the Back Bay of the Charles River which occupied Bostonians continuously from the 1850s through the 1890s. The creation of the present Seaport District began even earlier, but most of these 700 acres of Commonwealth Flats (as the area was called until recently) were created during the last two decades of the nineteenth century and first decade of the twentieth. The land on which Logan Airport sits represents another 750 acres of fill begun during the 1920s. In all some 3,500 acres of land have been created through more than a dozen major landfill initiatives spanning a 200-year period.

Among the remarkable waterfront environments that this land-making history produced are the Quincy Markets, an "urban renewal" project dating to the 1820s, and, as is well known, adapted and re-imagined by James Rouse in the 1970s as the first "festival market place." The Back Bay venture produced one of the nation's most distinctive residential districts, which during the 1930s was augmented as a riverfront environment by the construction of a portion of the Charles River Esplanade. Indeed, the Charles River was eventually graced by a continuous eighteen-mile-long public open space occupying both its Boston and Cambridge banks. Frederick Law Olmsted's late nineteenth-century work on Boston's park system produced Day Boulevard, Pleasure Bay and Marine Park, a continuous recreational open space along the southern and eastern edges of the South Boston Peninsula. Beginning in the 1960s Boston's oldest wharves, including Long Wharf, Central Wharf, Lewis Wharf, and a number of others in the North End, experienced adaptive reuse and/or reconstruction to achieve one of America's earliest transformations of obsolete maritime infrastructure and historic wharf architecture into modern waterfront residential neighborhoods.

So with such impressive achievements, both historic and recent, why is the planning of the Seaport District producing a crisis of confidence? And what, if anything, might Boston planners learn from the experience of the eight cities – Amsterdam, Bilbao, Genoa, Havana, Las Palmas, Shanghai, Sydney, and Vancouver – represented at the conference, many claiming to have been at least in part inspired by Boston's earlier waterfront successes?

As presentations of each city's waterfront-related plans or accomplishments proceeded some considerable overlap in sensibilities emerged. Despite great differences in location, city size, rates of growth, and, of course, the uniqueness of each society, these waterfront cities seemed to share the following conclusions/insights:

Along its waterfront, the aura of a city resides and persists

There is an enduring, even eternal, dimension to a city's waterfront as it bears witness – and often takes the brunt – of the ebbs and flows of a city's prosperity. Consider Shanghai. While Rome was not built in a day, it appears that Shanghai is determined to prove that it can be done. In a little over a century Shanghai has grown from a large fishing village to a megalopolis expected soon to reach twenty million people. The full ferocity of this barely imaginable rate of growth is being borne today. While Americans worry about sprawl, Shanghai seems to be building Manhattan and Los Angeles one on top of another. The Shanghai delegation at the conference described that, incredibly, 3,000 kilometers of elevated highways will be built in the metropolitan area over the next decade! With pride and without expressed sentimentality for the "good old days," so common today in the West, the delegation asserted that the transportation problem of the metropolis will be so solved.

Amidst such confidence for handling massive change can the DNA of the old fishing village survive, much less maintain relevance? Professor Zheng Shiling, vice-president of Tongji University, answered affirmatively as his colleagues presented a plan to reorient modern cosmopolitan Shanghai to its ancient river, the Huangpu, and to clean up its principal tributary, Suzhou Creek. While there will be many future highways, he said, there will only be one river. Precisely because everything in Shanghai is currently in flux, the re-commitment to its river is vital – and culturally reassuring. After all, Zheng Shiling concluded, "water reflects the morality and wisdom of our nationality." Such near mystical associations are not unique to Asian cultures and are valuable for waterfront planning anywhere.

Sure of their river as a stabilizing and enduring force and urban amenity, and welcoming modernization and growth, the planners in Shanghai are less concerned about precisely determining the most appropriate scale and uses along the river. In Boston, to the contrary, the general unease about the impact of further growth leads to a belief that certain uses, such as commercial office space and scale of construction (tall buildings), will forever damage a proper relationship of city to harbor. If Shanghai is too casual about development impacts, Bostonians may at the moment be too cautious about what constitutes proper waterfront development.

Despite undergoing periodic and sometimes rapid change, a waterfront maintains for its bordering city some inherent and unalterable stability

Mind-boggling though Shanghai's current growth is, the phenomenon is not unprecedented. Shanghai itself experienced a similar boom toward the end of the nineteenth century when its population exploded to nearly a million from around 50,000 at mid-century. By comparison to Shanghai, one thinks of Boston as being slow to change. Imagine then an expatriate returning to Boston following a forty-year absence, not so long a period in the life of a city. He would have left a Boston at mid-twentieth century with its historic waterfront emptying: a much-diminished port (partly relocated to the future Seaport District), abandoned maritime infrastructure, pollution and decay resulted in a sort of ever-receding land-side tide. The not-so-busy wharves were storing a different kind of commodity: parked cars for the downtown. The waterfronts of many industrial-era cities experienced a similar fate, and many have yet to recover.

Could our hypothetical expatriate have predicted that within a generation the bustle at the waterfront would return, not in the form of warehouses, custom houses, longshoremen or clipper ships, but by courtesy of homes, cultural institutions, tourists and pleasure craft. Boston's oldest waterfront is a center of action again, but in redefined uses and desires. Our expatriate would surely be surprised that Rowes, Burroughs, Lewis and Mercantile Wharves were now all elegant residential addresses, not places of industry; that life in the Charlestown Navy Yard was being directed by homeowners' associations instead of naval protocol; that forty-seven miles of shoreline were being steadily converted to a continuous public promenade; or that some of the most valuable local real estate was along the not-so-long-ago dilapidating wharves.

Despite such shocks to his mid-twentieth-century sensibilities, this returnee would have little trouble finding his way along Boston's historic waterfront. Amidst all that was lost or transformed sufficient continuity persists. The delegation from Amsterdam referred to such persistence as the "infrastructure" of the waterfront, and proceeded to show how it can be added to through imaginative new architecture and engineering. It is this capacity for persistence through reinterpretation that is one of the most valuable qualities of waterfront regions. This, too, should reassure Bostonians as they plan the Seaport District. They need only recall their own prior successful waterfront transformations.

A city's waterfront cannot be thought about as a thin line

One tends to think of land/water relationships in terms of opposites, or of the edge between the two. Metaphysically this edge is razor thin. In terms of city-building, the opposite is true. Places like Amsterdam or Sydney make this quite evident with their complex land and water weave. Even when geography offers less variation, the broader the zone of overlap between land and water the more successfully a city captures the benefits of its water assets.

It is generally easier to attract investment to the very edge, and over time construct (even overbuild) a façade to the water. The Bund in

Shanghai, the Malecón in Havana, the Avenita Marítima in Las Palmas; most cities possess at least one great linear avenue along their waterfronts (sometimes succumbing, sadly, to highway scale due to traffic). These avenues serve as prominent addresses, collect visitor accommodations and host celebratory events. They deserve much attention. Yet, nearly without exception the speakers at the conference spoke about resisting the allure of the "thin-line"; of approaching waterfront planning in terms of perpendiculars to the water's edge. The reason is that in most cities which have opted for a tall or dense edge of development at their waterfront, the value of land a block-or-two away from the edge drops precipitously, and with it the quality of the environment away from the water's edge.

Anne Cook, manager of Port Planning for the City of San Francisco, advised getting in to the water – both figuratively, by blurring the suddenness of the edge, and literally, by making sure that the remaining and potentially new industrial, transportation or recreational uses of the water sheet itself influence the land-side planning. Bostonians, for example, hold dear their "fingers-to-the-sea," the system of colonial streets (still prominent today) which were virtual extensions of the piers and wharves far into the Shawmut Peninsula. Developing the potential of such perpendiculars is often the key to comprehensive planning, more naturally resulting in both land-side and a water-side plans.

On this matter, several of the development proposals for the Seaport District deserve great scrutiny. The landowners nearest the water are, naturally, trying to maximize the value of their land by proposing to build tall; that is, upwards of 300 and 400 feet. Arguing substantial land carrying costs, and the demands of providing a variety of services – including streets and open space – which traditionally was the responsibility of the public sector, they insist that substantial height and density is needed to make construction and debt-service feasible. Avoiding the less desirable consequences of this thin, tall, dense line of development depends on the public's success in creating perpendicular streets and civic corridors which become considered equally desirable addresses.

There is long-term value to be regained; do not endanger this for short-term riches

One of the most poignant observations at the conference – pertaining directly to the seduction of the "thin line" – was made by Mario Coyula, the director of planning for the Havana capital region. Confronted with a dire need to improve (indeed, to create) an economy, and with international tourism offering a very tempting vehicle, Havana is struggling with how much of itself to offer and how quickly. "Do not lead with your best sites," Coyula advised, "the early investors want the best locations but do not do the best projects." How true this rings for cities which too quickly accept second-rate development proposals or engineer entire redevelopment plans around specific sites to enhance commercial real estate, or "jump-start" waterfront renewal.

Consider how unusual, and so far successful, Bilbao's efforts have been proceeding in reverse. First, and quite consciously, they set out to improve local self-esteem and enhance the region's image internationally through a cultural project, the Bilbao Guggenheim Museum. Now they are pursuing more conventional redevelopment efforts. Josu Bergara Etxebarria, the President of the Provincial Council of Bizkaia, spoke about the strategic goal of using culture as a tool for development, not just real estate development itself. The lesson here is that to compete globally may involve recasting, in some instances, rather than more narrowly preserving, a city's waterfront image.

Having achieved such recasting several times in its history, Bostonians have none the less approached the future of the Seaport District with quite conservative ambitions. The popular local imagination seems to prefer another Back Bay over visions of more innovative, future-oriented urban contexts. Unfortunately, the conditions under which the Back Bay was realized – incremental, block-by-block and house-by-house growth in which the public financed all services and the infrastructure, not to mention constructed the land – are not easily replicated today. But how to achieve similar results?

To make waterfronts come alive (after industry has receded) they must become places for people to dwell not just visit or recreate

Lord Mayor Sartor of Sydney spoke of the importance of maintaining a "living city" even as pressure to yield to financially more lucrative commercial development grows along thriving waterfronts. But the most impassioned support for housing at the water's edge was made by the Vancouver delegation whose "Living First" slogan hammered home the idea that residents are as important to cities as anything else. Some of the international participants may have thought this too obvious a point. Yet, taken within a North American context, where industrial-era cities have been shedding population to their suburban peripheries for half a century, it is a crucial insight. Starting in the 1980s Vancouver began the transformation of its many downtown waterfronts from industrial and rail uses with the goal of adding as many as 25,000 mid-to-high-density housing units, and by the century's end Vancouver was well on the way to achieving this goal.

The city's planning director, Larry Beasley, spoke of using waterfront locations to create a competitive advantage for downtown living against the allures of the suburbs. He called density, congestion and even high-rise housing "our friends" in creating lively, mixed-use urban lifestyles. He noted the city's adamant refusal to upgrade its highway system specifically to make it harder for people to commute from the periphery, thereby inducing them to select in-town housing. Until recently such talk would have seemed sheer lunacy in most American cities, and perhaps for many sound improbable still. Yet to experience Vancouver today is to understand what "living first" means: housing has here created demand for virtually everything else: new services, shopping and entertainment, public transportation, and open space.

The city as a place to dwell has been one of Boston's secrets too. Creating great places to live in the heart of Boston and Vancouver is held to be an early priority, not a later consequence of other actions. Curiously then, there is a recent concern in the emerging Seaport District that planning for much housing will crowd out other uses and privatize the waterfront. Those so concerned do not know their own city's history, or overlook that Boston's most urbane nineteenth-century accomplishment was to create the marvelous residential neighborhood of Back Bay, and as a consequence eventually gain a great public waterfront along the Charles River. Again, along its oldest waterfront at mid-twentieth century, Bostonians pioneered the American experience of adapting historic but abandoned maritime structures for residential uses. One can devise regulations against building massively, against the casting of undue shadows and loss of public access, but, in all but the most extreme circumstances of density (or incompatibility with still vital industrial uses), having more people living in the proximity of the waterfront is a long-term competitive advantage for a city. Rapacious users of land, as Americans unfortunately are, worry that only one thing may fit, but far more frequently than is assumed many uses can coexist side by side – especially across 700 acres of land.

Geography may be a significant road to and antidote from globalization

It was known for centuries as "Genoa the Superb," not because of its leading role in the seafaring culture of the Mediterranean but for its unforgettable silhouette as seen from the sea. The amphitheater-like form of the harbor appears carved from the coastal mountains, which in turn seem to emerge straight from the sea. While the historic harbor is no longer adequate in size for modern cargo shipping, its shape is even more powerful as a focusing device – like a centripetal force orienting the entire city to the old harbor. This condition of centering proved very useful as the city began to reinvent itself as a cultural and tourist destination in anticipation of the world-wide commemoration of the 500th anniversary of Colombus's discovery of America. In a prior epoch, geography enabled a well-scaled, well-protected port. Today it facilitates a diverse and spatially contained realm of contemporary businesses, institutional, residential and visitor facilities all in view of and surrounded by the layers of Genoa's prior lives.

Likewise, visits to Amsterdam, Sydney, or Vancouver – indeed, to many cities located on major bodies of water – leave indelible images of place. The value of these proverbial postcard views is not to be dismissed. As we begin the new century "globalization" represents, on the one hand, an ideal to reach (for cities and nations seeking access to the global economy) and, on the other, embarking on a road risking homogenization of culture and the loss of local identity. A memorable geography uniquely reinforced by a special pattern of urbanization can address both the ideal and the concern. A memorable setting can help attract global markets while forestalling the "this could be anywhere" syndrome of much current urban development. Just about every waterfront city should aspire to be called superb.

Perhaps unexpectedly, this is a greater challenge for Boston's Seaport District than in many cities. The original landfill created a rather featureless, very flat land form, far less dramatic than the contours of the South

Boston Peninsula to the east and that of the Shawmut Peninsula to the west. Thus, orchestrating a variable, interesting skyline may be more important than establishing some continuous district cornice heights (which some are advocating). As seen from the harbor the architecture of the district will have to compensate for the dull geography. Furthermore, the view *from* the Seaport District is generally toward an equally feature-less, flat, landfill-created landscape: that of Logan Airport immediately across the inner harbor. Views westward toward the downtown and east-ward toward South Boston, to the harbor islands and the open Atlantic beyond, are much more engaging (and come with less jet noise) than views directly across the water to the airport. It is interesting to contem-plate how the orientation of the blocks in the district – the massing of buildings and their architectural quality – could reflect these conditions. A standard "contextual" approach to the urbanism and architecture of the district may not produce a superb enough setting.

Along the waterfronts of cities world-wide, as well as in Boston, the human instincts both to preserve and to reinvent are robustly acted out in the passion play of waterfront revitalization. This dynamic is ongoing. Cities that at one moment successfully calibrate the imperatives of progress and those of preservation often face new challenges. The very attractions of a balance forged between progress and preservation bring additional pressures for change along valued domains such as waterfronts, threatening new harm to surviving evidence of the city's prior (even recent) epochs. Still, as Boston has shown over its three centuries, and will demon-strate again in its Seaport District, approaching this predicament with undue caution is rarely the best strategy. Perhaps the tactics of urban plan-ning at the waterfront should be a bit like that of the tide: scouring, reshaping, yet miraculously sustaining the shore.

Contributors

Richard Marshall

Richard A. Marshall is Assistant Professor of Urban Design at the Graduate School of Design at Harvard University, where he has taught since fall 1998. He teaches in core studio, Elements of Urban Design and Planning, which seeks to develop an awareness of the city as a complex physical organism; an organism that in whole and in innumerable parts is subject to analysis, planning, and design intervention. He also offers a seminar entitled "Emerging Urbanity," which explores the physical aspects of a series of large-scale urban developments in the Pacific Rim.

His current research effort is a comparative analysis of some ten Pacific Rim megaprojects. The work aims at an appreciation of the latent urbanity of these projects and speculates on the nature of how they manifest urban space and culture. The motivation for the work is that a critical evaluation needs to be made of the impact of new forms of homogeneity and heterogeneity on the contemporary condition of the city.

Marshall is an Australian architect and urban designer. He is a member of the Royal Australian Institute of Architects. His professional experience lies in urban design and master-planning projects, in the design of commercial high-rise office projects, high-rise residential buildings, and educational projects. His experience covers projects in Australia, Singapore, Malaysia, Indonesia, China, and Thailand. He was a senior designer with the Japanese firm Nikken Sekkei, based in Singapore, before joining Woods Bagot to become the manager of their Kuala Lumpur practice.

Marshall has authored articles on urban-design-related topics. He has spoken at international conferences, notably the OZONE Living Design Center in Tokyo to start a series of seminars and an exhibition on sustainability in design in 2000, and 1º Fórum Internacional de Urbanismo, entitled "New Visions for the Boston Waterfront" at a conference entitled Requalifacação de Margens Ribeirinhas com Envolventes Urbanas, at Univeridade de Trás-os-Montes e Alto Douro, Villa Real, Portugal in 1999.

His forthcoming book, also by Spon, deals with the nature of contemporary urban projects in the Pacific Rim and places them in a larger understanding of contemporary urbanism. He received his B.Arch. Studies and B.Arch.(Hons) from the University of Adelaide, Australia, and his MAUD from the GSD. Richard Marshall was the faculty coordinator for the conference entitled Waterfronts in Post-Industrial Countries, held October 7–9, 1999 at the GSD.

Rinio Bruttomesso

Rinio Bruttomesso is the Director of the International Center for Cities on Water and a Professor of Urban Design at the University Institute of Architecture in Venice. He is also the editor of *Aquapolis*, an international review that deals with waterfront-related developments and issues.

Bruttomesso is the author of many publications on water-related development, including *Waterfronts: A New Frontier for Cities on the Water* (1993), *Cities on Water and Transport* (1995), *Urban Waterfront Redevelopment in Italian Cities. Case Studies: Genoa and Venice* (1995), *Urban Waterfront Transport in the Framework of a Complex Interchange* (1996), and *Land–Water Intermodal Terminals* (1998).

He has spoken, and continues to speak, at numerous conferences, seminars, and round tables throughout the world, notably the First and Second International Conferences of Aquapolises in Osaka and Shanghai respectively, the 1996 and 1997 Asia Pacific Waterfront and Marina Development Conferences in Singapore and Cape Town, the Forum Europa Nostra in Naples in 1998, and the Italian Institute of Culture in Sydney in 1998.

He is a member of the board of the International Association of Aquapolises in Osaka, the International Waterborne Transport Sub-Committee, the UITP (International Union of Public Transport, Brussels), and of ASM-Venice Mobility Services Company.

Anne Cook

Anne Cook is Manager of Port Planning and Development (Waterfront Development) for the Port of San Francisco. Her role is to oversee port development projects to ensure better utilization of property consistent with the Waterfront Land Use Plan and to ensure that projects are acceptable from a financial, regulatory and community standpoint. Cook has extensive experience from both the public and private sectors, having worked as a land use, real estate and local government attorney before moving into planning and project development.

Prior to her appointment as Manager of Port Planning, she was Manager of Regulatory and Environmental Affairs (Waterfront Planning), responsible for all long-range land use planning of port-controlled property from Fisherman's Wharf to India Basin.

Cook graduated *cum laude* from the University of California, obtained her Master in City Planning degree from the Massachusetts Institute of Technology, and obtained her degree in Law from University of California, Boalt Hall School of Law. She was admitted to the California Bar in 1987.

Alex Krieger

Alex Krieger, FAIA, is Professor in Practice of Urban Design and Chairman of the Department of Urban Planning and Design. He also serves as

Director of the Urban Design Degree Programs, which include the Master of Architecture in Urban Design and Master of Landscape Architecture in Urban Design.

He is a founding principal of Chan Krieger & Associates, where ongoing professional projects under his design direction include the Carl J. Shapiro Clinical Center at Boston's Beth Israel Deaconess Medical Center; new athletic facilities for the Buckingham Browne & Nichols School in Cambridge; the Discovery Museum in Bridgeport, Connecticut; Boston's Congress Street Bridge; campus plans for the Rhode Island School of Design, Harvard University, the Harvard Medical School, Knox College in Galesburg, Illinois, and Deerfield Academy; master plans for Boston's City Hall Plaza and environs, downtown Cincinnati, downtown Worcester, downtown Minneapolis, and downtown Des Moines; and design reviews for the Harvard School of Public Health, Northeastern University and Dartmouth College.

The firm's work has received prizes in eight national competitions, two Progressive Architecture awards, and three AIA awards. Krieger has authored five monographs, including *Design Primer for Towns and Cities* and *Towns and Town Making Principles*.

Krieger serves as the director of the National Endowment for the Arts' Mayors' Institute on City Design, was one of the founding members of the Boston Civic Design Commission, serves as the design review architect for the Providence Capital Center Commission, and is an adviser to the Boston Redevelopment Authority on various downtown planning and design projects. His master plan for the Central Artery corridor was one of eighteen projects in the Urban Revisions exhibition organized by the Museum of Contemporary Art, Los Angeles, which recently returned from a two-year tour of North American museums.

Martin L. Millspaugh

Martin L. Millspaugh was in charge of the development of Baltimore's world-renowned Inner Harbor waterfront from 1965 to 1985. For the past fourteen years he has been involved in consulting on mixed-use real estate developments for private and public property owners on five continents.

He is an author and columnist and lecturer, and has served as Assistant Commissioner in charge of research and development for the Federal Urban Renewal Administration.

From 1965 to 1985, Millspaugh was Chief Executive of the public–private development corporation that he created to act as the "delivery mechanism" for Baltimore's Charles Center and Inner Harbor redevelopment plans. Both projects received the Award of Excellence from the Urban Land Institute. The Inner Harbor was honored by the American Institute of Architects as "one of the supreme achievements of large-scale urban design and development in U.S. history." In all, these two projects have received forty-two national and international awards for excellence in planning, design or execution.

Millspaugh received the Distinguished Service Award of the US Housing and Home Finance Agency (now HUD) in 1960. In 1981 he was selected by the Greater Baltimore Committee to receive its Annual Award for Civic

Achievement. In 1996, he was named an honorary member of the Urban Land Institute, where he serves as a member of the Forum on Regionalism and the International Council. He is a member of the Board of Directors of the World Trade Center Institute and serves on the Advisory Boards of the National Aquarium in Baltimore and the Real Estate Institute of Johns Hopkins University.

Since 1985, Millspaugh has been Executive Vice-President, then President, and now Vice-Chairman of the Enterprise Development Company and Enterprise Real Estate Services, Inc. Both companies are for-profit consulting and development firms participating in mixed-use, leisure and entertainment-driven development projects in the US and overseas.

Alden Raine

Alden S. Raine is a consultant in urban development and transportation, whose current assignments include the $400 million Providence Place Mall, station area development along San Juan's Tren Urbano corridor, and the redevelopment of Springfield's historic Union Station. From 1991–1993, Raine was Executive Director of the Massachusetts Port Authority; from 1983–1990 he was the state's Director of Economic Development and Chairman of the Governor's Development Cabinet. He has played a key role in the clean-up and redevelopment of Boston Harbor, in Boston's other "mega-projects" (Artery-Tunnel, North and South Stations, Southwest Corridor, Logan Airport modernization), and in city-building projects throughout Massachusetts. Raine graduated from Harvard College, received a Ph.D. in Political Science from the University of Michigan, and taught at Rutgers and Clark Universities.

Barry Shaw

Barry Shaw is the Chief Executive of the North Architecture Centre and consultant on town planning, urban regeneration and conservation planning. He is currently expanding the role of the Kent Architecture Centre, its services and expertise, in view of the UK government's emphasis on urban renaissance.

He is a member of the English Heritage London Advisory Committee, and a member of the committee advising the Department of Culture? Media and Sport (DCMS) on the remit for the Commission for Architecture and the Built Environment; is Visiting Critic at Harvard University Graduate School of Design, Unit for Housing and Urbanization; from 1993–1996 he was a Board Member of the Tower Hamlets Housing Action Trust; and formerly Head of Urban Design for London Docklands Development Corporation responsible for the design direction of Greenland Dock, Surrey Quays and Butlers Wharf – projects that have taken seventeen national and international awards. He was previously responsible for establishing the London Borough of Southwark Surrey Docks Team, following work as an architect planner with Milton Keynes Development Corporation.

Alfonso Vegara

Alfonso Vegara Gómez is President of Fundacion Metropoli, Madrid, Spain, and Director of Proyecto-CITIES, an investigation of the competitive advantages and the factors that constitute the success of twenty innovative global cities.

Vegara is the author of several publications including: *El Proyecto Urbano*, *La Ordenación Urbana*, *Urbanismo de Ideas*, *Madrid Metrópoli*, *El Triángulo Alicante-Elche-Santa Pola*, *Logroño, Programa Ciudad*, *Innovación y Desarrollo de Ciudades y Regiones*, *La Ordenación del Territorio del País Vasco*, and *La Ordenación del Territorio de las Islas Baleares*.

Vegara is President of the Taller de Ideas Group, based in Madrid, Spain, and has directed a number of urban and regional planning projects including the Regional Plan of the Basque Country 1990–1995.

Index

Page numbers in *italic* refer to illustrations.